ENTICING
HARD-TO-REACH
WRITERS

ENTICING
HARD-TO-REACH
WRITERS

RUTH AYRES

STENHOUSE PUBLISHERS
PORTLAND, MAINE

Stenhouse Publishers
www.stenhouse.com

Figure 1.2: Created by Factoryjoe, used under CC BY-SA 3.0

Every effort has been made to contact copyright holders and students for permission to reproduce borrowed material. We regret any oversights that may have occurred and will be pleased to rectify them in subsequent reprints of the work.

Library of Congress Cataloging-in-Publication Data

Names: Ayres, Ruth, 1977- author.
Title: Enticing hard-to-reach writers / Ruth Ayres.
Description: Portland, Maine : Stenhouse Publishers, 2017. | Includes
  bibliographical references.
Identifiers: LCCN 2017016462 (print) | LCCN 2017039325 (ebook) | ISBN
  9781625310910 (ebook) | ISBN 9781625310903 (pbk. : alk. paper)
Subjects: LCSH: English language--Composition and exercises--Study and
  teaching--Psychological aspects. | Composition (Language arts)--Study and
  teaching--Psychological aspects. | Creative writing--Therapeutic use. |
  Education--Biographical methods | Narrative therapy. | Children with
  social disabilities--Education.
Classification: LCC LB1631 (ebook) | LCC LB1631 .A75 2017 (print) | DDC
  808/.0420712--dc23
LC record available at https://lccn.loc.gov/2017016462

Cover and interior design by Tom Morgan (www.bluedes.com)

Manufactured in the United States of America

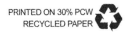

PRINTED ON 30% PCW
RECYCLED PAPER

23 22 21 20 19 18 17   9 8 7 6 5 4 3 2 1

For my own kids who started in hard places, because they are proof that we can always rewrite the way our stories go. Hannah, Steph, Jay, and Sam, I'm so glad I get to be your mom.

Contents

Acknowledgments

There are a few people who see the stories I carry around inside of me a little clearer than the rest of the world does. People often ask me how I manage to do so much. It's because of the people who see my beautiful mess of a story and aren't afraid to walk along with me.

Becca and Lee go out to dinner with us every month. They know how to muster a little more energy to go out at the end of a week that's been full of bad news, funeral eulogies, and disappointments. Even when it makes more sense to cancel, we show up, a little tattered, and eat dinner, have a drink, and laugh. Becca, no one fields frantic texts and late-night phone calls better than you. Thanks for always reminding me that there's more to me than walking the hard road of healing children from trauma.

Jas and Trev have six kids in their home right now: two biological kids, one adopted kid, two about-to-be-adopted kids, and one foster kid. They know what it's like to live with kids who come from dark places. They know adoption isn't a fairy tale. They are a phone call away from picking someone up from practice, coming over to help with a temper tantrum, or canning two bushels of peaches so they don't spoil when you are overwhelmed because your kid has just been arrested and you're supposed to be meeting a writing deadline. They make walking alongside kids from hard places seem a little less insane.

There are people who have taken this tangle of words and helped spin it into a book. Ruth Metcalfe, my writing partner, said, "You're on the black diamond slope of parenting." There's a good chance Ruth has read this manuscript more than I have. It's because of her that it makes sense. You wouldn't have wanted to read the mess that came before. I wouldn't want to write without her.

Bill, my editor, told me to keep going. I might have whined (more than once) and stumbled and reached out for a hand to help me find my footing. Mostly he said, "Keep going." There was one phone conversation when I was sure he was going to tell me it was over, but instead he said, "You're writing a lyrical essay. Keep. Going."

It's a good thing I had my computer open and could google "lyrical essay" to find out what it was. Panicked, I turned to Wikipedia: "Lyrical essay is a contemporary creative nonfiction form that combines qualities of poetry, essay, memoir, and research writing, while also breaking the boundaries of the traditional five-paragraph essay."

I sighed and beamed. Bill said, "I like the way you write about your family."

I kept going.

I have friends around the globe who encourage me to keep writing. They like the way I work the words, they like my stories, and they affirm that I write universal truth. Thank you, Elsie (Leanne Carpenter), Christy Rush-Levine, Deb Day, Linda Baie, Kim Barrett, Ramona Behnke, Tara Smith, Jen Vincent, Leigh Ann Eck, and Patrick Allen.

There are writing friends a little closer to my corner of the world. We meet and laugh, and they tell me my stories matter. This book wouldn't exist without Ruth, Tam Hess, Tammy Shultz, and Mary Helen Gensch.

I also have a summer writing group thanks to Brenda Power and the Choice Literacy Writing Retreat. Franki, Katie, Cathy, and Max, thanks for the walks and the talks. They make me a better writer. Brenda, you keep me going when I think I should quit.

Family comes in all kinds of containers. Mom, Dad, and my "little" brother, Jeff, taught me early on that family are the people who love you to be yourself. I have a school family. Wawasee is a special place to work. It is a corporation that uplifts people and provides both roots and wings. I wouldn't be the educator I am if I landed somewhere else. Thank you, Joy Goshert and Tom Edington, for allowing me to fly. If you are part of the Wawasee family, I am grateful for you. A special thanks to the All-Write Consortium for the cutting-edge professional development brought straight to our backyard. I have a great school community and get to serve on the local school board. It's awesome. I adore my church family . . . especially the high school Sunday school class, which I have the privilege to teach.

The stories that make up this book wouldn't exist without those who share breathing space with me day in and day out. This year, Andy and I returned to our respective college campuses to show off our old stomping grounds to our children. If someone had told us then that all of these kids would call us Mom and Dad, we would have laughed big belly laughs. This zany family is beyond our wildest imaginations. Taija, Kari, and Marty, thanks for expanding our understanding of family to include the whole globe. You are each my favorite host daughter ever. Hannah, Stephanie, Jordan, and Sam, you are my sunshine. Andy, I love you, and I really love loving people alongside you. It matters that we *turn darkness into light*.

Mostly, thank you, reader. Thank you for following my stories as I blog and for being E-mail Pals on my newsletter and for fluttering around social media with me. I hope you have people who see your beautiful mess of a story and aren't afraid to walk with you. You need them if you are going to help heal children from dark places.

INTRODUCTION

"**D**ad, there are some things I need for first grade; can we do some shopping?" our daughter Stephanie insisted. Stephanie is always insistent. She and Andy were standing outside a dollar store, and even though he sensed he was being taken advantage of, he decided to go with it.

"Sure," he said, holding the door open for her. "How much money do you need?"

Stephanie stepped through the door and put her hands on her hips. She surveyed the store. "Two dollars," she said with authority. She is always in charge, which is why her nickname is The Boss. She is proud of this name, and we use it with affection.

Andy unfolded his wallet and gave The Boss two dollar bills. Stephanie clenched the bills in her fist. "Don't worry, Dad, I'm going to use this money for things I need. I want candy, but I'm not going to buy it. I'm going to buy what I need for first grade."

She scouted the aisles, assessed the possibilities, then retraced her steps. On the third pass, Andy said, "You should decide soon."

"I know what I need. I'm getting it now."

They paid for the items and walked out of the store. "Thanks, Dad!" Stephanie said, lifting her shopping bag above her head with one hand and holding Andy's hand with her other. "Now I am totally ready for first grade tomorrow."

Andy smirked at me when they came home. Stephanie announced, "Dad took me shopping so I could get the things I need for first grade tomorrow."

Andy's nods and wide eyes exaggerated his innocence, and his too-big grin foreshadowed trouble.

"You already took your supplies to school. You have everything you need," I said.

"Not everything," Andy said, his grin widening.

Stephanie placed her shopping bag on the counter. "Sometimes you don't know what you need until you need it," she said, opening the bag and proudly holding up her purchases. "These are just what I need for first grade!"

"I agree," Andy said. "You wouldn't ever have known you needed those things for first grade."

"Andy!" I exclaimed, "She can't take those to first grade!"

Stephanie put her hands on her hips. "I *need* them, Mom!"

Andy nodded his head in support of Stephanie. "C'mon, she *needs* them!"

"I can't believe you bought those for her." Andy winked at me over the top of Stephanie's head.

"Dad didn't buy them for me, I bought them. Dad just gave me money." I looked at our daughter, her hands on her hips and her blue eyes insistent. "Please, Mom, I really need these for first grade tomorrow."

I'm pretty sure Stephanie was the only person to bring fake fingernails and handcuffs to school the next day.

This was both the beginning and the end of Andy overseeing school shopping. Why Stephanie ever "needed" fake fingernails and handcuffs for first grade escapes us now. What matters is that we recognized Stephanie had a need and we filled it.

It's not always fun to meet Stephanie's needs. This happens when kids come from hard places. When Stephanie was eighteen months old and her sister Hannah was four years old, they were removed from their biological family and spent two and a half years in a foster home with a single Amish woman and six younger foster children. In 2008, parental rights of the girls' biological parents were terminated. Stephanie and Hannah were ready to be placed with a forever family.

I'm not sure why we received the call. They met all three requirements on our "never going to adopt" list:

Sibling set of girls.

One was in kindergarten.

The other had anger issues.

At the time, we had a two-year-old son. We adopted Sam after we'd been married long enough for people to stop asking if we were going to have kids. Sam's birth mother was incredibly generous and invited us to be present for his first moments. I cut the umbilical cord after he was born. His birth mother placed Sam in our arms. We held him and counted his ten toes and touched his soft fingers and were enamored by his eyelashes and the way he breathed gently in and out. He was fresh to the world.

No babies or toddlers are easier to care for than Sam was. He rarely cried, never soiled his clothes, and slept through the night by the time he was six weeks old. He learned to smile and laugh big belly laughs from his tiny belly. Sam loved to observe the world and spent hours watching toys spin and tree leaves sway to figure out how the world worked. We joke that he was reading a book when he arrived in the world. He has always been an avid reader.

Most importantly, he was born with the uncanny ability to make people feel loved.

When we decided to become licensed foster parents, our priority was to keep Sam safe. If there were going to be siblings, we wanted one to be a boy. If they were going to be older, then we didn't want them to be in school. (The outcome is grim for children who are not adopted before they start kindergarten.) Finally, we would not take any child who had anger issues. We needed to keep Sam safe.

The call came; ten days later, we became a family of five. I was a momma to the world's most easygoing toddler, a kindergartner who was a professional at using the nurse pass, and a four-year-old who attended a therapeutic preschool for children with anger issues. At the time, I didn't even know there were enough children with severe anger issues to merit a whole preschool program. (I understand if you need to read that again: one of my new daughters attended a therapeutic preschool for three-, four-, and five-year-old children with *anger* issues.)

Hannah was six. She exhausted every possible pitch to go to the nurse in the first eight months of her school career. For Hannah, survival was about finding love by being needy. Unlike Stephanie, she rarely threw fits. In fact, Hannah was kicked out of the therapeutic preschool because she wasn't angry enough.

There was a time when I enjoyed *not knowing* there was a need for therapeutic preschools. It is heart-wrenching to think about children that young with severe anger issues. Sometimes when things sting our hearts we stop thinking about them. Who wants to think about young children with anger issues? Certainly not this momma.

And definitely not this educator. I became a teacher to change the world. Isn't this why we all become teachers? We want to change the world by offering an education to every child. We want children to know they can grow up to do anything. When their anger issues are so severe that they have to attend therapeutic preschools, it's a lot harder to believe that education will change the world.

Each year, our classrooms are filled with children from hard places. Their needs are overwhelming. They are hungry. They need shoes. They need a place to sleep. They need heat. They need safety. They are living in meth labs. They are living in cars. They are living in fallen barns and abandoned buildings. I knew kids would come from hard places when I started teaching and before I became a momma, but I didn't realize it took more than a big heart to erase the "hard."

I had all kinds of knowledge back then and lots of big ideas. My whole life was preparation for becoming a teacher. When I was a little girl, I'd barter with my brother: I'd play He-Man and Skeletor with him if he played school with me and did some of the assignments I, the teacher, gave to him, the student who always demanded more recess.

I spent my teenage years babysitting during the school year and working as a camp counselor in the summer. I learned to have fun with kids, to listen without judgment, and to encourage others to live the best version of their stories possible.

Despite my efforts to become something else—an architect, a physical therapist, a biologist—eventually, I found myself with a piece of paper declaring a bachelor of science in education with a major in biology and a minor in English. I also found myself in a middle school classroom where I was responsible for teaching readers and writers. Within weeks, I was frustrated and discouraged as a teacher. I was killing the love of reading and writing each day with my stupid language arts class. Kids were either shouting out answers (and insults) or slumped in their desks sleeping. The world was not becoming better by me being a teacher.

It was easier to let kids sleep than to wake them up. Midterms went home and my dreams of being a teacher were turning to nightmares. I worked after dismissal, and lost track of time in my windowless classroom.

One day, a soft knock on my classroom door startled me. It was long after my colleagues had said goodbye for the day. I looked up from my too-big desk to see a man in the opposite corner of the room.

"Mrs. Ayres?" he asked. He was in a work uniform—gray pants, gray belt, gray boots, and a gray shirt. There was a white oval patch above the left pocket with his name in gray script. I wish I could remember what it was.

I stood up and walked across the room. I offered my hand. As he shook it, I noticed his eyes were gray, too.

He pulled a piece of paper out of his back pocket and unfolded it.

"My boy brought this home," he said. He turned the paper so I could see it was a midterm report. In the grades column, one stood out from the rest.

F.

I traced the line back from the failing grade and saw my name and course listed. It felt like an accusation, even though the man did not blame me and was not angry.

"I'm glad you came to talk with me," I said.

He looked behind him, and I saw my student, Rheece, in the shadows of the hall. "Come on in," said the man, inviting Rheece into the room. Rheece's younger brother followed, too.

The man stood between his boys and put his hand on Rheece's shoulder. He said, "What happened? He's never failed a class."

I looked at Rheece. His eyes were on the carpet.

"He sleeps through class," I said.

"Do you wake him up?"

My eyes wanted to stare at the same spot on the carpet as Rheece. Instead, I looked the man in the eyes and said, "No."

He took a deep breath and seemed to get grayer. "Why didn't you wake him? Language arts is important."

It was a fair question, and my answer seemed inadequate. "I decided if he didn't care and wasn't causing a disruption, then it wasn't my job to stop him."

The man's eyes turned a darker gray. It was like watching the sky churn before a storm, getting darker as the potential for devastation increases.

"You're a teacher," he said in quiet voice. The words cut deep into my heart.

My eyes widened. The storm began to swirl. I looked at Rheece with his eyes down and his shoulders slumped. His brother took a small step toward him. The trio stood before me. They all shared the same gray eyes.

"I'm sorry," I said.

"If you would have called me," he said. "We could have done something. Because of this F, he can't play football. It was the one good thing happening in our lives. Rheece plays football and I don't have to worry about him getting in trouble before I get off work. Rheece plays football and has a reason to keep his grades up. Rheece plays football and Nick and I sit in the stands and cheer for the team. Rheece plays football and we have something to talk about when we sit down to dinner. Now Rheece isn't allowed to play football."

"I'm sorry," I repeated.

"Why didn't you just call me?"

The words were in my brain, but couldn't get past my sliced-open heart. *I didn't think you would care.* I said "I'm sorry" a third time. The words sounded more like an excuse than an apology.

"Well, maybe this midterm will teach us all a hard lesson," the man said, folding up the midterm and sliding it back into his pocket. "If I had known, then we could have made some changes. Rheece still needs to get his work done. Please send home his incomplete assignments, and I'll make sure he does the work."

I nodded.

"Mrs. Ayres, you should know that Rheece is doing the best he can. We're just having a rough time right now. His mom left. She didn't say goodbye. She just didn't come home one night or the next night or the next. It's been enough nights that we're realizing she's probably not going to ever come home."

He squeezed both his boys' shoulders. "We're doing the best we can. In the future, please don't let Rheece sleep through your class."

A fourth time: "I'm sorry." They were the truest words I could speak. I felt small.

I had all kinds of knowledge, but I was still unprepared. That midterm taught me a hard lesson, but it would be more than a decade before I completely understood the way a teacher makes the difference for kids or families just doing the best they can.

There are dark corners of this world, and "hard" comes in all different forms. For Rheece's family, it was his mom leaving. For me, it was adopting older children from foster care.

Being a mom to a baby fresh to the world is very different than being a mom to children who have been scraped by the world's ugliness. When children come from hard places, they learn to protect themselves. Rheece slept through my class not because he didn't care about school, but because he was surviving the hard of life. Stephanie developed anger issues not because she was an evil child, but because she was surviving the hard of life. Hannah went to the nurse and demanded attention not because she was manipulative, but because she was surviving the hard of life.

It took me five years to find my footing as a momma to daughters who lived their first years in dark corners of the world. Just like Rheece, I checked out. I quit maintaining friendships. I quit exercising. I quit cooking from scratch. I buried myself in writing. We were doing the best we could, and I survived. But barely.

When I finally emerged, with a stronger spirit than before, we decided to adopt another child. No one was more surprised by this choice than Andy and I. In 2013, we adopted our fourth child, Jordan. Sam called him Jay, because "Ayres boys shorten their names." The shortened version remains.

Jay made us a transracial family of six. After spending seven years in the foster care system, Jay came home to our forever family just before his eighth birthday. He had seen the worst of humanity in foster care. But Jay is a survivor. His smile makes you smile back, and his life makes you believe in the power of possibility. He is a living story, rewriting the beginning into something better—just like our whole family is.

In this book, I entwine my three story lines as educator, momma, and writer. As an educator, I know the research behind how kids learn, instructional strategies, and classroom management techniques. As a momma, I know the meaning of trauma and stress beyond a textbook definition. I understand the way a history of hard impacts a child. I've seen the way a brain is altered when a child isn't nourished. And as a writer, I know the inner workings of building a story. I know that all stories have struggles and how the hero wins in the end. More importantly, I know how to help children rewrite their stories into an account of survival and courage, and I know how to hold their hands as they heal—*wholly* heal—and live out their remarkable stories.

To write this book, I let my story lines of educator, momma, and writer whisper to one another. I wanted to convey how to cultivate the stories and messages of young writers so they can bloom, making the world a better and more beautiful place.

In Part I, I explore the way trauma changes brains, but also delve into the truth that brains can heal. Learning how to apply recent brain research will help us wrap strong arms around children from hard places and give them a chance to rewrite their stories. We will also consider the impact social media has on students' life stories.

In Part II, I discuss the importance of enticing all students to write. Not just those who are reluctant or inexperienced—we *all* need to be enticed to make our voices heard in a big world. And we must learn not only to write stories, but also to communicate information and opinions that allow darkness to turn to light in this world.

In Part III, I share seven leaps of faith for teachers. These practical suggestions will entice all writers to write regardless of their struggles.

There are whole stories bumping around our schools that we don't know. Even if we did know them, we probably wouldn't understand them. What we *do* know is that no matter who you are, life is sometimes hard. The little girl who demanded fake fingernails and handcuffs is now in seventh grade. Like most teenagers, she needs things that we don't understand.

As I write this, our kids are in grades five, six, seven, and nine. We run them to marching band, basketball, football, Cub Scouts, bowling league, youth group, and friends' houses. We go to games, band and choir concerts, and school and church events. We cook together in the kitchen and gather around the table for dinner. We tell stories around the campfire, and we can still all fit on the same couch for a rare bedtime story. We also are hosting a year-long exchange student: Martha is seventeen and from Norway, but lived in Eritrea the first half of her life. She is already part of our forever family, just as our previous exchange students, Karianne and Taija. Our days are filled to the brim.

Just as my family has changed over the years, so has my teaching life. That conversation with Rheece's dad spoke to my heart. I took his words—"You're a teacher"—seriously and figured out how to refuse to give up on any student.

But first I had to figure out how to stop destroying readers and writers. My journey led me to best practices and workshop teaching, transforming my work. I was having so much fun meeting the challenge of growing readers and writers that I never wanted to leave the classroom, but I did. Eventually I became a district

FIGURE I
Our family in chalk.

instructional writing coach. I planned to support teachers in their writing instruction for a year (maybe two) and then return to my own classroom.

I did the job for a dozen years.

Currently I am an Innovation Specialist for the same school district where I started as a rookie teacher. I coordinate elementary instructional coaching as well as other professional development to foster inquiry and innovation. After all these years, one thing remains the same: I help people—staff and students—know that their stories matter. The core of my professional life is encouraging others to use their voices to change the world.

It takes a whole community to help a child heal. I know because I've seen healing in my own kids. Andy and I are not enough to meet their needs; they need others. Given the trauma they have faced, Andy and I often do not understand their choices, nor do we understand the things they need. Many of our parenting moves are as crazy as buying a first grader fake fingernails and handcuffs to take to school.

The kids' classroom teachers have expedited their healing, but it will take a long time for them to recover and write happy endings to their stories. As an educator, I spend my days with kids from hard places. You do, too. We don't always know what they need. Sometimes we don't even know the traumas they are living with. Often it is impossible. Unlike my own children, many of these children are still living in dark corners.

It's our job as teachers to help students see the positive impact they can have on the world. You may be the only person to help the children in your classroom know they can write their stories in any direction they choose. For many kids, teachers are the last hope for healing.

I collected the stories of my own children and curated the research that follows as my offering to you. May you find it possible to fill needs in your corner of the world, even when it seems like fake fingernails and handcuffs might be more of a help.

PART I

HOLDING ON IN THE HARD: UNDERSTANDING KIDS WHO NEED TO BE ENTICED TO WRITE

CHAPTER 1:
STORIES SAVE

n college, I became a brain research junkie. I blame my dad, an elite pistol shooter who believed in practice and mental toughness. His mantra was (and remains): *What you think is what you get.* I was alive for three decades before I realized it was Henry Ford—not my dad—who said, "If you think you can or you think you can't—you're right."

I majored in biology with the intent of becoming a brain researcher. I loved saying the names of the parts of the brain—*cerebellum, hippocampus, thalamus, amygdala.* Go ahead and say them aloud, allowing them to roll off your tongue. Who wouldn't become addicted?

I collected brain facts the way my college roommate collected office supplies—copiously and compulsively. Of all the information I was absorbing, what tugged at me most was how dependent brains are on nourishment. I was drawn to the ancient debate of nurture or nature. I wrote research papers and spent hours, days even, in the library stacks.

My love of brain research led me to an adolescent development course, which steered me to becoming a middle school teacher. It seemed like the perfect career for me—building relationships with young adolescents, teaching about a subject I enjoyed, and working alongside complex developing brains.

Even after graduating and accepting a teaching position, I continued studying the brain, piling on as many adolescent development classes as possible and

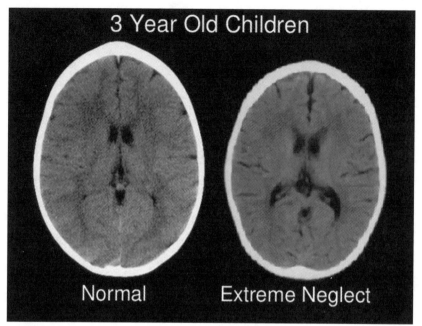

FIGURE 1.1
Images from Dr. Bruce Perry's research about brain nourishment

reading any professional book I could get my hands on about teaching with the brain in mind.

Then we adopted Hannah and Stephanie from foster care. It turns out brain researchers have a lot to say about adopted children, most of it grim—so I quit reading brain research. I closed my favorite books and didn't open them again for a long time.

Just like the start of a new school year with students, there is a "honeymoon period" when you adopt children. I remember the day we first brought the girls home. Andy and I opened the coat closet to show the girls where they could put their shoes when they entered the house. They nodded, and Stephanie smiled at her mint-green bucket. "Do you want some help taking off your shoes?" I asked.

"No," Stephanie said.

"Okay, then take off your shoes and put them in your bucket."

"No," Stephanie said.

I slipped Sam's shoes off. He toddled to his blue bucket and dropped them in, then went off to play with his train set. Hannah put her shoes in her bucket as well and joined Sam to play.

Stephanie just folded her arms and jutted out her chin.

The honeymoon was about to end. I always thought they lasted more than a couple of minutes.

I bent down to untie Stephanie's shoes. "I'll help you," I said.

"No!" she screamed. I pulled my hands away from her shoe strings.

"No!" she screamed again, stomping her feet this time. I stood up.

"No!" She threw herself on the floor. I stepped away.

Andy and I just stood there, watching her throw the ugliest fit we'd ever seen. I caught Andy's eyes across the entryway; he was grinning his silly new-dad grin. I was petrified. This was the shortest honeymoon period in existence. Stephanie slept in her shoes that night.

Images of Dr. Bruce Perry's cross-sections of brains from his research about brain nourishment began to haunt me. (See Figure 1.1) I was learning how to parent a four-year-old with anger issues. We started timing Stephanie's meltdowns and found that they happened about every seven minutes.

Children need love and solid boundaries. We used to celebrate when Stephanie had just ten meltdowns before lunch, and eventually worked our way to less. After eighteen months, there were some days without a single meltdown before lunch. We focused on love and boundaries; I kept ignoring all I knew about the brain.

Although Stephanie's basic needs were being met and her meltdowns were decreasing, she still exhibited extreme defiance and threw ugly fits. I decided to ignore Maslow's hierarchy of needs (see Figure 1.2) along with all of the other brain research I was burying in the pits of my mind.

But ignoring something doesn't make it go away.

Ignoring something doesn't make it untrue.

And ignoring something doesn't make healing happen.

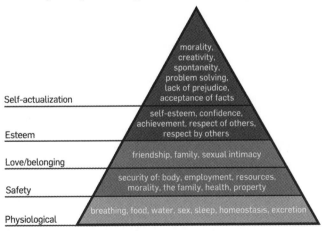

FIGURE 1.2
Maslow's hierarchy of needs shows basic needs must be met before humans engage in creativity.

The truth is that children's brains *are* altered when they experience stress and trauma. Dr. Perry's cross-sections in Figure 1.1 show this. Both brains are from three-year-old children at opposite ends of the nourishment spectrum, and the differences are stark. The well-nourished brain is larger with a thicker membrane, whereas the undernourished one is smaller and the dark spot in the center representing the amygdala is enlarged.

The amygdala is our emotional control panel. It is the part of the brain in charge of feelings, emotional behavior, and motivation. Fear is the primary emotion in children from hard places, and the amygdala is where fear forms.

Stephanie survived the first years of her life by learning to take care of herself. Although everything in her early years was unpredictable, she figured out ways to be in control. By screaming, flailing her arms, and kicking, she could get her own way. She didn't talk until after the age of four, yet fully potty-trained herself before the age of one.

Stephanie has more willpower than most and learned soon in life that if she wanted something done, she would have to do it herself or with the help of her sister, Hannah. When most children were playing on swings, Hannah and Stephanie were sleeping through the night underneath a park bench. When most toddlers were learning to eat cut-up grapes and broccoli, Hannah and Stephanie were digging through trash cans for leftovers. When most children were wrapped in a favorite warm blanket for naptime, Hannah and Stephanie were cuddled in a closet in a house without heat.

They lived in fear. Fear of being hurt. Fear of being cold. Fear of being hungry. Fear.

All.

The.

Time.

Living like this alters the way a brain develops. The girls' amygdalae became enlarged.

When a neighbor reported to the authorities that Hannah and Stephanie were living in a home without heat, the girls were moved into a foster home. They were fortunate to have a safe foster home; many children don't. Though Hannah and Stephanie were living in a safe home, their emotional control panels had been altered. Not only was their default emotional response fear, but their emotional control panels were wired to react extremely.

Stephanie chose loud anger and aggression. Hannah chose sweet lies and manipulation. Though their journey through foster care was a best-case scenario and they ended up with us, changing the environment is not enough to heal the brains of children with such extreme challenges. This was a hard truth for me to accept. The adoption placement team told us all the horror stories of Stephanie's anger issues; they didn't sugar-coat anything. In fact, they purposely painted a grim picture. Andy and I listened and were indignant when one woman said, "If you decide to go through with the adoption, it is supposed to be forever. When it gets hard, many people want to return the children to the system. This is not ideal for the children."

Andy spoke firmly, "We believe family is forever. Once we adopt the girls, they will never be returned to the system." Even then, knowing what we knew about the hard history of the girls, there was a part of both Andy and me that believed things would automatically improve by changing environments.

Environment and circumstances do influence a child. So do altered amygdalae. It doesn't matter if there's a shoe bucket in the front closet and a warm bed upstairs, the child will still feel fear first and most strongly. If we are going to help children rewrite their histories of hard into stories of hope, then we need to develop new thinking paths in the brain. The way to do this is to short-circuit fear.

CHAPTER 2:
ALTERED BRAINS

FEAR, NOT WILLFUL DISOBEDIENCE

As discussed in Chapter 1, fear is the primary emotion for many children. This was hard for me to believe until I lived with kids whose go-to emotion was fear. To complicate matters even more, children mask fear with anger, anxiety, and apathy. As I learned to recognize behavior stemming from fear rather than defiance, I noticed more and more children who seemed to be living with this emotion.

Think of a student in your classroom who doesn't want to write. Take some time to visualize the child. Imagine where he is sitting. Imagine what she is wearing. Look at his feet. Notice her hands. Where is he looking? What is she doing?

More than likely, the image you conjured does not include a pencil. This is often the first characteristic teachers list when asked to describe a child who doesn't want to write—no pencil. We've all faced kids without pencils. Some may even go most of the writing time undetected because they are quiet and have writing folders and paper and everything else that lead us to believe they are writing—except they're not, because they have nothing to write with.

You know what happens next. You ask, "Where's your pencil?"

Take a moment and imagine how your student responds.

Maybe you cringe when you hear yourself asking the question, because you know the child is going to yell back. There might even be pounding fists and shoving chairs. You are shocked by the overreaction to a simple question. The child is responding with *fight*.

Another kind of response is withdrawal. The student sinks back, inching under a table or pulling up a hoodie and trying to disappear. The child is responding with *flight*.

Some children stare back. Their faces are blank, and other than a few blinks, they have no reaction. The child is responding with *freeze*.

Fight, flight, and freeze are common responses to fear. It's important to realize that when we think children are being willful, they may actually be afraid.

TRADING GOOD FOR BEST

When I read brain research as an undergrad, the ideas of Jensen, Glasser, and Sousa made sense—but parenting children with enlarged amygdalae has made the black words on white pages become all the more real. This isn't just information found in books; it is reality.

I've decided to stop asking "Where's your pencil?" in class. I understand that it's good for students to develop responsibility by keeping track of their writing supplies. Responsibility for supplies is a life skill. But I've decided to trade what's *good* for what's *best*.

It's best to meet needs. Students who are not afraid ask for a pencil when they don't have one. The lesson ends, they gather their supplies, and when they realize they don't have a pencil, they ask a neighbor or a friend or the teacher, find a pencil, settle in, and start writing.

Children who are afraid to ask for a pencil, by contrast, may be *doing their best* to stay safe. Life experiences have taught them that if they ask for something, they may get in trouble. They have learned not to depend on adults to meet their needs, so they *do the best they can with what they've got*. They gather all the supplies they do have and then they *do their best* to blend in—to look like writers. They aren't trying to cause problems; they are *doing their best*.

This is true for our son Jay. He is good at remaining unnoticed when he doesn't have the supplies he needs or when he doesn't know how to do something. Jay's first life experiences taught him that it is best to remain unnoticed. It took Andy and me a little while to figure this out.

Here's a typical scenario. Jay comes home from school and sits at the table with the other kids to do his homework. Andy pours them each a glass of milk. As soon as he sits it at the table, Jay buckles down and focuses on his work. The other kids chat about school while they work, but Jay blocks them out.

When the kids are all done, they depart and leave their homework on the table for us to check. The kids who were joking and chatting the entire time usually have all their assignments completed correctly. All too often, Jay's homework is absent. He has a talent for sidetracking us when we ask for it, so there are many nights when his homework doesn't get checked. We don't realize until we get his report card that although he does end up reliably turning in his homework, his answers are all incorrect.

When we talk with Jay about his homework, the conversation goes in circles.

"Jay, it is important to do your best on homework."

"I am doing my best."

"You are turning in homework with zero correct answers."

"Why do you want me to always be perfect?"

"Doing your best on homework is not about perfection. When you do your best, you take the time to do things correctly."

"I am doing my best."

And so on. It's been a paradigm shift for me to realize that people who are *doing their best* aren't necessarily behaving within social norms. This is because I've always lived in a world where my needs have been met. When I *do my best*, it is so that I can operate at the peak of Maslow's hierarchy of needs. Students in my classroom whose needs have *not* been met must trust me to meet their needs if they are to do *their* best—so if they don't have a pencil, I'm going to give them one rather than castigate them. My priority is to meet their physical needs so they can grow as writers.

Let's return to the student in your classroom. What if instead of asking "Where's your pencil?" you said this:

"You look like you're ready to work as a writer. Good job gathering most of your supplies! I see you still need a pencil. Do you know where to find one?"

The student may respond with fight, flight, or freeze—a harsh "Duh," a shrug, or nothing at all. No matter the response, keep your focus on meeting the student's immediate need. This is the only way you can begin to build trust. Continue:

"One thing you can do is ask someone to borrow a pencil. If you ask some people around you and still can't find a pencil, ask me. Writers need pencils, and I'll always loan you one."

When we provide for the needs of our students, we prove to them they are valuable and worthy. Respect students enough to believe they are doing their best as writers. If they need a pencil, give them a pencil.

A SYSTEM TO KEEP PENCILS

You're probably wondering if I own a pencil company. The primary reason we don't give out pencils, of course, is that we tend not to get them back. When I was a first-year teacher, I forced students to swap shoes for pencils. I'm sorry, but I did. Students would leave their shoes by my desk in exchange for a writing utensil. It was a stinky deal in more ways than one.

When I give students pencils, I show that I respect them enough to help them meet their needs. When I take their shoes in exchange—well, that's just a shoe for a pencil, and then they have to limp for the rest of the day. (Unless, of course, they lose the pencil they borrowed and have to swap their second shoe as well.) I send the message that although I have the resources students need, I'll only share them at a cost. For students to overcome fear, their needs must be met without strings attached. We need them to learn that we care about them as people. It was Theodore Roosevelt who said, "Nobody cares how much you know until they know how much you care."

I don't believe kids lose pencils on purpose, but I do believe they are grateful when they have the resources they need to do the work. To help students out while also keeping track of my supplies, I started putting little masking-tape flags on my pencils that read, "Help! I'm missing my home. Please return to our writing center!" I kept a big batch of these pencils in a cup in the writing center. Though I still lost pencils, I did so at a much slower rate.

One day, a student brought a flowerpot to class filled with dried beans and fake flowers taped to the tops of pens. Even kids who remembered to bring pencils would use these flower-pens for writing. Today my daughters make duct-tape flowers as pen-toppers. It doesn't really matter how you mark your pencils, just that you mark them in a big, loud way so they are easy to spot and return. If a student returns a pencil a few days after borrowing it, be glad that you got it back, not crabby that it took a while.

The only way you can empower students to write is to become the kind of person they can trust to meet their needs. If they can't trust you to find them a pencil, how will they trust you with their stories? Providing resources for resistant writers is the best way to get them to soften up and bravely face the blank page.

GOT RESOURCES, BUT STILL NO WORK

Of course, giving a kid a pencil isn't necessarily going to produce Nobel Prize–worthy writing. It's more of a circular process: Some days words will be written, some days there will be other needs to meet, and some days you're going to give out more pencils.

I fight the battle to entice every student to write because I know that sharing our stories makes the world a better place. Learning to write allows kids from all walks of life to have a stronger grasp of their futures and dreams. As educators, we must understand that when students fight they aren't being angry, when they flee they aren't being defiant, and when they freeze they aren't being lazy. Their brains have been altered by trauma, and it takes a long time to help a brain heal.

CHAPTER 3:
TAKE TIME

E arly in Jay's fifth-grade year, we received a series of e-mails from his math teacher. Math is Jay's best subject, but the teacher was concerned about his ability to focus in class and get along with other students.

One day when Andy and I were putting away laundry, we raised our concerns.

"This is a problem, Jay," I said. "What are we going to do about it?"

We made sure it was a casual conversation—Jay doesn't need the added stress of worrying about getting in trouble. We kept the conversation light because we knew Jay wasn't being distracted on purpose. He wasn't being malicious by not listening. And he didn't delete all those slides in the group project because he wanted to be a big jerk.

"Why did you delete the slides?" Andy asked.

Jay shrugged and murmured, "I don't know."

It's so easy for him to pull away from us. He shifts his position, physically turning away. It takes time for children to learn we are on their side.

We pulled the story of the deleted slides out of him bit by bit. It turned out that Jay was upset because the other two people in the group were doing all the work and he felt left out. He wanted to do part of the project, but didn't know how. What he had learned over the course of more than six years in foster care, though, was how to get attention. So he started deleting the slides. Things went downhill from there.

Jay's eyes welled with tears. "I just wanted to help," he said, swiping his cheeks with his palm.

Andy said, "Did you ask the group, 'What can I do to help?'"

Jay picked at a thread on the comforter. He shrugged.

"If you want to help, sometimes you just need to ask what to do."

"I didn't think of that," Jay said.

Andy patted his back. "When you want to help, then ask to help. It always goes better than making the work difficult."

"That makes sense," Jay said. I turned to hang up another shirt so he couldn't see my smile. It's a simple concept, but one he hasn't learned. Most of his life has been about survival, rather than learning about how to get along with others.

"I'll try to stay focused and get along in class."

"Sounds good," we said. We hugged him and he went outside with his football.

Jay has experienced trauma for most of his life that has altered his brain, making it difficult for him to pay attention. His class wasn't given directions on how to collaborate as a group, so he reverted to doing what he knows gets attention: irritating others.

When tragedy strikes, people are quick to extend grace. We all have examples from our own lives of times when we altered our decisions based on events. When I was rear-ended on my way to work, I wasn't reprimanded for being late; when a friend's mom was in the hospital, I didn't expect her to meet me for our usual walk; when Sam broke his collarbone, his baseball team adjusted the batting lineup and sent him a gift card to Dairy Queen. People understand that trauma is a game changer and we respond with empathy.

Just because a child's trauma is in the past doesn't mean teachers shouldn't alter their expectations accordingly. If my son walks into your classroom, you wouldn't "see" the tragedy; you'd notice his neon socks and his bright-red high-top kicks. He'd smile and you wouldn't be able to stop yourself from smiling back.

You wouldn't know by looking at Jay, or by looking at his family, that he's experienced years of trauma and tragedy. He will be sixteen years old before he's lived more of his life with us than without us. He has seen the very worst of humanity, but covers up this knowledge with trendy clothes, a winning smile, and great hair.

Once class starts, though, you'll start noticing all the ways trauma has influenced Jay. He'll drum his fingers and swing his legs, kicking the desk in front of him. He'll stare out the window, ignore your directions, and leave his work uncompleted.

If you had Jay in your class, you'd want to talk with his parents. You'd tell us that he doesn't focus and that he's a poor time manager. I've been on both sides of the table for this discussion. As a teacher, I wanted parents to understand what their children were doing in class. At the time, I would have said I was "maintaining parent-teacher communication." Now that I'm on the other side of the table, I realize that although my intentions were kind, they were not helpful.

Sitting on the parent side of the table across from one of Jay's fifth-grade teachers, I'm not sure how to respond. She has piles of incomplete work, lists of poor behaviors, and the assignments clearly lined up on the right side of the board. She shows us her clear directions and the work of other students and explains expectations for the standardized test. She sums up her case with the last punch: "I wanted to meet so you can give me insight about how to get Jay to focus."

I'm sure our blank stares are not what she's hoping for. "It's too much," I say. "He is overwhelmed by the different assignments and the amount of tasks he has to get done. Even I'm not able to keep it straight."

"This is what all fifth graders are expected to do. It is very organized and laid out for him. He just needs to learn to focus. He is a very poor time manager."

I'm silent and take a slow breath, trying to push back the tears and control my temper. I attempt, again, to explain that Jay's brain is different than those of children who have been emotionally nourished for their entire lives.

She cuts me off. "So what you're saying is you don't have a solution? You can't tell me how to get him to stay on task?"

The conversation is not satisfying for either side of the table. The teacher wants a quick solution (and I don't blame her), and we want Jay not to be overwhelmed. She wants Jay to be successful. She cares about his success. She's taken the time to meet with us. Ultimately, though, until she understands that trauma altered Jay's brain, it is unlikely she will be able to help him.

Less than two weeks later we meet with the teacher again, this time in the principal's office. We are glad the principal is going to join us, but we can't help but wonder how most parents would feel about meeting with the teacher in the principal's office. We don't feel warmly welcomed. We feel like we were failures as parents.

Things are still going downhill for Jay. Although we spend hours helping him with his math homework every night, it still isn't meeting the teacher's expectations. Now he is being assigned to the "Catch-Up Room" during lunch and recess: Instead of relaxing with friends and burning energy on the playground, he sits at a desk correcting his homework. It's the same homework that takes hours of our family time each night, but because it's not formatted to the teacher's specifications, Jay has to redo it during lunch.

To Jay's teacher, he just needs to learn to manage his time. She doesn't understand how the trauma of his early years makes it hard for him to do the things she asks. She's trying hard to help Jay, but it isn't working, and we don't know how to explain why. We aren't living up to the teacher's expectations of supporting our child's schoolwork at home, and we're struggling to advocate for his needs.

"We know he's still not focusing," Andy says. "It's one of the crummy things he has to deal with because of the junk that happened in the first eight years of his life."

"By this time of the year, we expect him to be completing his homework the way we explain it in class," says the teacher. "If he's not, he's going to go to the Catch-Up Room for help.

"Today he left the room to find my co-teacher," she continues. "She asked me, 'Where did you send Jay?' I was worried about him. No one gave him permission to leave. He just left! He wasn't angry; he just decided to walk out of the classroom. We went to the hallway to look for him and he was heading back into the room. 'Where were you?' I asked him."

Andy chuckles. This story is typical Jay. The teacher says, "Jay told me he was 'looking for the other teacher.' We stared at him and said, 'She's in the room!'"

I smile and shake my head. Andy says, "That's what we mean when we say he's not focused. He isn't doing it to be difficult. His brain works differently than other kids' do. He thinks he can take care of things himself—like finding the other teacher. Or he feels threatened or overwhelmed and he checks out. He's overwhelmed with all of the math assignments."

"I have all of his assignments outlined here on the grade sheet," says the teacher. "I also have them posted in the classroom. He just has to decide what to do and do it." It feels like a broken record, repeating the same conversation over and over and over.

"It's not working," I say. "This isn't working. It's too much."

The principal lifts the needle off the record, ending the repetition. "Can you give Jay one assignment, and when he completes it, give him another assignment?"

"I've already done that," says the teacher. "Here's the list. He just has to choose."

I'm exasperated. Thankfully I keep my mouth closed.

"What I think they're saying is the choice is overwhelming for Jay," says the principal. "Can you make the choice for him? Then when he finishes, give him the next assignment—your choice, not his."

"If you tell him how long it should take to complete the assignment, I think that would help him, too," I add. "He likes to time things."

Andy smiles. "Yeah, he really loves his watch."

The teacher thinks for a moment. "So even though the assignments are all on the board, he's still feeling overwhelmed."

We nod. "You know, I just realized something," I say. "At home, if we give Jay a single chore to do, he does it very well. But if we give him three tasks to do, he doesn't do any of them well. I think it's the same thing. He's overwhelmed by the choice." As Donald Graves said, "Unlimited choice is no choice at all." This is wise advice for learning to meet the needs of kids from hard places.

Jay has a difficult time focusing. This shouldn't be a surprise; it should be expected. Yet even I, his mom, sometimes forget the effect that trauma has had on him. It's no surprise, then, that teachers must work to remember this as well.

CHAPTER 4:
HEALING HAPPENS

Scientists are finding that when children are nourished by intentional adults, their brains can heal. My own children have been removed from hard places and now live in a forever family that nourishes and invests in them. They spend their days with educators who nourish and invest in them. They have coaches and a church family who nourish and invest in them. They are healing because of the positive relationships in their lives.

It is a process. In our experience, the process is not quick, nor is it easy. In fact, it seems to be one tangled mess of a little bit of progress and a whole lot of falling back into old habits and thought patterns and behaviors. If this is true for our children, who have an entire community nourishing and investing in them, then it's not a stretch to believe that it will take even longer for children who are still living in hard places.

There are moments, days, sometimes even months when Andy and I think our children have finally overcome their rough starts to life. Then we stumble over manipulation or stealing or lies, and we realize it's not about a destination. It's not as though one morning our children will suddenly wake up free from the nightmares of their first starts in life. It's unfair to expect healing to work that way. It is, rather, a lifelong journey.

This is true for each of us, not just children facing difficult circumstances. We are *all* changing. This is life—constant change. The intent is to move toward better versions of ourselves. Some legs of the journey are filled with tremendous growth—we achieve and build and succeed again and again. These are the sweet spots on the trail—the path is clear, the wildflowers bloom, the rainbows glisten. Other legs of the journey are like hairpin curves that double back on themselves, as though no progress is being made at all. We plod ahead, wondering if we are getting anywhere.

It's not the trail that can be changed, it's us. Jay can't ever "un-live" what happened to him. Hannah and Stephanie will never have baby pictures of being cuddled while rocked to sleep. These legs of their journeys are unchangeable. We can't keep mothers from drinking or fathers from going to jail. We can't stop cancer or mental illness. Every trail has unavoidable obstacles. But we, the travelers, can develop endurance and learn to thrive.

About a year after Hannah joins our forever family, I'm tucking her into bed when she says, "I wish I could be reborn."

Her words give me pause. "Will you say more about that?" I ask.

"Well," she says, "Sam's lucky because he's always been here. That makes him easy to love and he loves people back super easy. I'm not lucky. If I were reborn with you as my mom when I was a baby, then I'd be lucky, too."

"You aren't unlucky, Hannah. You are special and we love you."

"The memories I have don't feel very good. I wish I was reborn and could live like Sam." Hannah's voice is muffled by the plump comforter she's pulled up past her nose.

I used to wish I had a magic wand that would take away all of Hannah's hurt, but the truth is she is who she is because of her experiences. They aren't fodder for sweet bedtime picture books, but they are a foundation for her to develop the perseverance to overcome hardship. Learning to change her story is much more powerful than the wave of a magic wand.

Hannah is not unlucky, not unlovable, and not bad at loving people back. She is a survivor who loved her little sister so much she took care of her and helped her become a survivor, too. This is the story I recount for Hannah.

"Do you remember how you used to sleep next to Stephanie when she was a baby in order to keep her warm?"

She nods. "I gave her bottles, too."

I smile. "I know. You were really good at loving her. You still are. Remember how you gave her some of your dessert tonight at dinner?"

She giggles. "She really loves sweets!"

Although the process of helping a brain heal is trying and slow, it's not complex. Brains heal in the same way they are nourished at the beginning of life: by having their needs met. If children from hard places know their needs are going to be met in the classroom, their brains begin to heal and they are able to put words on paper.

The act of putting words on paper is itself healing. Writing is not only necessary for students to learn to communicate well, it's also highly therapeutic—and writing workshop is at the heart of helping children learn both its academic and emotional benefits.

Children need writing like they need air. It helps them become well-rounded and secure in themselves, to touch hearts, to use their voices for social change. We need future doctors, software developers, foresters, journalists, biologists, engineers, graphic artists, teachers, web developers, dental hygienists, accountants, architects, plumbers, florists, pilots, and business owners who understand how to use English properly and offer their stories, interests, and knowledge to affect the world for good. Every single student has an important story to offer the world. As teachers, we are on the front lines of rescuing and setting these stories in motion.

Most children, even those without hard histories, experience stress. A death in the family, parental job loss, moving, health concerns, severe weather events—all of these affect brain development. We have the opportunity to make our schools sanctuaries from the hard of life. When we nourish students at school, they are able to relax. They don't have to wonder if they will be warm or have something to eat or be punished for making a mistake. When school becomes a refuge and children's needs are met, brains begin to heal.

EVERYONE WANTS TO BE THE HERO

Every story has a hero. *The Princess Bride* has Inigo Montoya. *The Wizard of Oz* has Dorothy. *Star Wars* has Luke Skywalker. We all want to be the heroes of our own stories. By showing kids how to become the heroes of theirs, we can help them to heal. It's what I did for Hannah when she whispered, "I wish I could be reborn." I placed her as the brave and compassionate hero protecting her little sister.

Today, Hannah doesn't remember asking to be reborn when she was seven. She reads the draft of the scene and smiles.

"You and Dad have a louder voice in my brain than the stuff that happened before we were a forever family," she says. "Sometimes my brain tells me one thing, but then I think about what you guys would say and I know what's true."

The thing about heroes is they always have a guide. Inigo Montoya had Fezic. Dorothy had Glinda the Good Witch. Luke had Yoda. To help students rewrite their stories, we must be their guides. I love the scene in *The Wizard of Oz* where Dorothy meets the Wicked Witch of the West and snags the ruby slippers. Glinda guides Dorothy. We can learn a lot from Glinda about how to be an effective guide. (Scan the

 QR code here to go to the scene where Glinda the Good Witch meets Dorothy for the first time and take a moment to notice how she serves as Dorothy's guide.)

Let's consider the qualities of a guide based on your favorite story. Think of a familiar plot from a book or movie. Then open your notebook (paper or digital), set a timer for seven minutes, and quick-write using the following questions as inspiration:

- *Who is a guide in your life?*
- *What qualities of a guide do you see in Glinda?*
- *Who is the hero of your favorite story?*
- *Who is the guide?*
- *What are the guide's actions?*
- *How are you inspired by the guide?*

Each time I lead this exercise, I'm enamored by the favorite story lines selected. Even more remarkable are the commonalities between the guides. *Harry Potter, Pretty Woman, Finding Nemo,* and *Gladiato*r all have guides who serve as solid inspiration for empowering the hero.

Humans are wired as storytellers. Our brains use story to make sense of the world. Unfortunately, the stories children tell themselves are too often inaccurate. When kids live with these untrue stories it impacts their behavior (academically and emotionally) in the classroom. When we go from seeing misbehavior as willful to seeing it as a chance to meet needs and build relationships, we position ourselves to act as guides for our students, helping them shape their stories. It is essential for us as teachers to help them put words on the page so they can see the true story they are living.

CHAPTER 5:
SEE THEIR STORIES

P icture a glass jar filled with your favorite pens. Imagine every color of pen inside the jar—red and turquoise, ocean blue and fuchsia, sunshine yellow and neon orange. There are also some dark pens—navy and black and grey and brown. This jar is like the students in our classrooms: They each carry around inside of them a beautiful story, with a handful of dark spots.

My friend Becca Snider, a mental health therapist, first gave me the idea of a jar of crayons to represent students. Becca taught me that behaviors often mask the stories of children who come from hard places.

When I lead workshops, I like to conduct the following exercise, which Becca developed, to make this abstract idea concrete. I ask teachers, What do students do or say when they don't want to write? Then, I write the responses with a marker on strips of duct tape and tape them to a jar full of crayons. Soon enough, the pretty jar is entirely covered with ugly tape. The same is true for the writers in our classrooms: Their behaviors cover their stories.

I've come to believe that enticing writers is about peeling off the strips of tape to see the story underneath. When I meet a student's basic need, I'm able to pick off a bit of the tape. It's not easy; sometimes it takes more than one attempt to peel the tape off the jar. Sometimes I have to meet the same need so many times I think I'm going to pull my hair out. I keep at it, though, because the work is too important.

It matters that students learn to use their voices to tell their stories, share their passions, and advocate for their beliefs. As Chris Crutcher notes in *Adolescent Literacy,* "Teachers save lives" (Beers et al. 2007, 16). Our classrooms may be the last place where healing is possible for some students. Writing workshop may be the only opportunity for their voices to be heard. This school year is the best time for all students to be nourished and to write their stories in directions that make their voices matter and the world better.

CHAPTER 6: GETTING THE HEART RIGHT: SOCIAL MEDIA AND STORIES

The phone sits between my teenage daughter and me on the table as we enter another discussion about digital responsibility, or "do the right thing with your tech." The conversation is already getting old and she's only had her phone for a year. This scares me, since there are three more soon-to-be teenagers living in our house. I'm not sure how to help Hannah learn digital citizenship.

She does things that make my blood boil. She texts me demands. She's rude to her friends. She posts pictures with revealing information. She chats with strangers during English class. I remind myself that she needs to go through this learning process and that it's a good thing she's learning to make wise choices with her phone. At the same time, I want to hide the device until she's thirty-seven and isn't compelled to send seventeen messages in two minutes to her crush. (Yes, I know, only "old people" say *crush*.)

What makes my head spin is that she's really a great kid. She's thoughtful and considerate. She does the dishes and folds the laundry. She always does her homework on time and she communicates meetings and schedules like an adult. She is a classic oldest child—until she gets a phone in her hand. Then her brain turns to mush.

We're bumping along through this together. Hannah is learning how to live a story partly through social media, and I'm learning how to empower her to share her story while at the same time protecting her from harm.

Social media alters our stories. When my youngest son, Sam, turned nine, he started censoring what I posted on social media. Sometimes I'll snap a picture and he'll say, "Don't post that on Instagram."

I'll smile and respond, "Oh, come on, it's really cute."

His face stays straight: "I don't do cute on social media." (He has also informed me that his childhood stuffed animal, Ducky, doesn't have a signed photo release, so he is never, under any circumstances, allowed to be seen online.)

By contrast, Jay will sometimes say, "Mom, come take a video of this for Mamaw. You can post it on Twitter, too. Your followers will love it!" He has a sense of sharing our stories with family in another state as well as with a larger, global audience through my Twitter feed.

Our classrooms are full of kids who know there are stories on social media and who want to join in. Many of them already have: Each year, more and more children are connecting to social media networks. These networks function as digital texts, allowing students to tell their stories through tweets and Instagram posts. No longer are stories confined to lined paper.

Students need strong guides as they share their stories online, especially because digital texts require practically no processing time between idea and publication. Although social media has the incredible ability to connect and affect the world for the better, it also has the power to harm.

THE STRUGGLE BETWEEN LIGHT AND DARKNESS

At the beginning of her eighth-grade year, Hannah sends eighty-seven e-mail messages over the course of a forty-two-minute English class. The next day, she sends another ninety-four e-mail messages during the same class. If you do the math, that's over four e-mails per minute.

Hannah isn't caught sending these high-tech notes during class. Even more mind-boggling, the school filters don't flag the content of her e-mails. Most disturbing of all, she is mentally checking out of English class while maintaining an A-plus course grade.

One night, well after Hannah's bedtime, a series of bells starts ringing. When we check to see what it is, we find a long list of e-mail notifications on the screen of Hannah's school-issued iPad. I check her e-mail history and I'm floored by the amount of sent messages I find.

It's not Hannah's finest moment, but I think middle school is a whole season of not our finest moments. The stakes are higher now, though, because technology is involved. When I was in middle school, I had to handwrite that nasty note to another girl. I had to fold it up and keep it in my pocket so the teacher wouldn't find it and read it in front of the whole class. I had to think about the best time to deliver it and then arrange to be in the right place at the right time. By the time I finished writing the note, I was usually calm enough to think rationally. I would tear the note into itty-bitty pieces, scattering it into trashcans throughout the school.

Many kids today have a compulsive response to digital texts. They send and receive massive amounts of data. They post on social media and check every few minutes to see whether they've gotten any comments, add to the discussion, or fret about the lack of response. This compulsion affects their story lines. They judge the quality of their own narratives based on whether they receive responses to their posts.

Feedback has the power to be helpful or hurtful. The potential for good online is vast—but so is the potential for devastation. We must figure out how to empower the former and protect from the latter.

Because it's late at night when we realize how many e-mails Hannah is sending and receiving during English class, we don't yank her out of bed and yell at her. Instead, we wait until after school the next day to have a quiet conversation.

"So Hannah, we noticed you sent a lot of e-mails during English class these past few days."

Hannah has the same fierce look as her momma when she doesn't like what she's just heard. "Why were you reading my e-mail?" Her voice is as sharp as her eyes.

The conversation isn't loud, but it is long. We're walking through uncharted territory. My parents never had a conversation with me about sending too many e-mails or text messages, or about how digital texts form imprints that can never be removed. My parents never had a conversation with me about being addicted to technology.

Hannah doesn't even remember the things she wrote. I start reading her e-mails aloud.

"Stop! Just stop!" she cries.

"What's the matter?" Andy asks.

Her tears fall freely, dropping off her nose and plunking down her cheeks. "I hate the way I sound. I didn't mean all those things. I don't want to be that kind of person."

A parent's heart can be ripped out by a child's remorse. "Come over here with us," says Andy.

Hannah leaps from her chair to sit between us on the couch. She folds into us and sobs. "I don't want to be like that. I wasn't even thinking." She heaves and keeps her face buried. "Please don't read any more. Just get rid of it."

"It doesn't go away," I tell her.

"Delete it," she says, her voice scratchy.

"It's your school e-mail; it's already backed up. That's how things work, Hannah. If you share something digitally, you can't be guaranteed it'll be deleted."

Hannah's not the first teenager in the history of teens to make a poor choice. She's not the first teenager to say things she didn't mean or to be sucked into drama. She is, however, among the first generation to experience the consequences of these decisions online.

"If you were smoking cigarettes, we'd take away the cigarettes," says Andy.

"I'm not going to smoke cigarettes," she snaps.

"We think you need to learn to use technology in a safe way."

Hannah looks at her hands. "I'm afraid I can't control myself with e-mail. If it's there, I'm going to use it to stir drama."

And this is the reason I share Hannah's not-so-fine moment with you: because it leads to this moment of pure resilience. The fibers of her being are cut from a cloth of survival and perseverance.

We could simply discipline Hannah for her poor choice. She would be mad, the consequence would come to an end, and she would repeat the same mistake. Instead, we have a conversation and dig around to find the root of the matter.

"What do you think we should do?" I ask her.

Hannah is silent. She's a thinker. "I can't really get rid of my iPad since school gave it to me," she says. "I can leave it in my locker for the classes I know I won't need to use it in. For the other classes, I can give it to a friend to hold until we need to use it for class work."

I love the way she takes responsibility for her actions. It's a good plan, but ultimately, we decide it isn't fair to expect another eighth grader to hold Hannah accountable.

Hannah starts crying again as she shares another plan. "We can ask the school to put me in digital dungeon." Her tears flow faster.

"Digital dungeon?" Andy chuckles.

"It's not funny, Dad. That's when they lock your iPad so you can't e-mail other students and you can't get online. That's probably what I need them to do."

Isn't she amazing? I'm reminded that none of us are ever all good or all bad. There's a little bit of light and darkness in each of us. Hannah is growing up to become the kind of person who admits her shortcomings and is willing to make sacrifices to overcome them. A bright light shines from her.

"Tomorrow we'll go into the school and ask them to lock your e-mail, but leave your online access open."

"Will I get in trouble for the e-mails I sent?"

"Probably, so it's best to admit it and accept the consequences."

Her tears come back. "I don't want to be the kind of person who does this stuff."

"Then stop. Set boundaries so you won't do these things."

She takes another shaky breath and stops crying.

"It'll be okay," Andy says.

Hannah nods and the tears start up again. Her words tumble out too fast, as though she has to get them out as quickly as possible or they might not come out at all.

"If I'm going to stop stirring drama and stuff, then I probably need to give up my phone too. I'm not using it the way I should. I'm obsessed with it and keep sneaking it when I'm not supposed to have it. And I know I'm over-texting. I don't want to give it up, but I think I should. I'd be healthier."

What'd I tell you? She's remarkable. At the close of this chapter, it's not the copious e-mails you will remember about Hannah, but rather her resilience as she fights to be a better version of herself. This is possible because she is given a conversation alongside the consequences. Technology isn't a stark black-and-white world; it is shades of dark and light, depending on the stories we choose to tell.

As guides on a digital journey, we must travel ahead of our students and get to know the path before they reach it. Most teachers are connected to social media in their personal lives; if you're not, knock on the door of the teacher across the hall and ask him or her to help you get connected to an online platform that many of your students' parents also use.

Here are three keys to becoming a successful guide for your students as they learn to tell their stories using technology:

1. *Create a social media account for your classroom. Make sure it is separate from your personal account; it's important to draw bold boundaries around your professional and personal life.*

2. *Keep your posts positive and useful. Not everything that happens in a classroom ought to be plastered on social media. Focus on celebrations and share snippets from throughout the day. Make selections that will be most useful for parents to know.*

3. *Be consistent. You will connect with parents most when the content and timing of your posts are predictable. Share information that highlights a variety of classroom experiences, making sure to connect to all families.*

TOUCHING HEARTS

In thinking of guiding students through social media, I'm reminded of a passage from the middle-grade novel *A Crooked Kind of Perfect* (2009) by Linda Urban. The book has nothing to do with digital citizenship, but everything to do with being the kind of kid who is secure in her story. Zoe, the main character, wants to be a concert pianist more than anything, but she has to make do with being an organist because her father has bought her an organ that comes with six months of lessons. At the Perform-O-Rama competition, Zoe realizes music is not just about getting the notes right, but it's about the heart, too. Urban writes:

> *Perfection itself is imperfection.*
>
> *That's what [Vladimir] Horowitz said.*
>
> *I heard it on that show I watched with my mom. The voice-over guy said that Horowitz meant that it wasn't enough to get all the notes right. When you play the piano, you have to get the heart right. Which is harder than getting the notes right.*
>
> *Each note can only be right in one way. A B-flat is a B-flat is a B-flat. A robot can get a B-flat right.*
>
> *But getting the heart right is something only a person can do. And the ways to do it are as many and as different as there are people in the world. (165)*

Writing workshop is not just about getting the instruction right. It's not about a canned program, or a great app, or a lockstep process. It's about getting the heart right. Enticing writers is about touching hearts and taking leaps of faith to pull all students into the possibilities awaiting them when they learn to write well.

PART II

SETTING THE STAGE TO ENTICE STUDENTS TO WRITE

CHAPTER 7:
WHAT WRITING
HAS TO DO WITH
TEACHING WRITERS

I t's my first year of teaching, and our staff is reading Harry Wong's book *The First Days of School* (2004) and watching his video series. In the very first pages of the book, Wong describes the following stages of teaching: Fantasy, Survival, Mastery, and Impact. He cites Kevin Ryan, who conducted research about these phases of teaching and concluded that most teachers never make it past the Survival stage.

I laugh along with my colleagues as we watch Wong describe the Fantasy stage in one of his videos. Two weeks into the school year, I'm thinking, "No way am I in Fantasy. I love my job and love building relationships with students. I just know what a great job it is." (It's okay for you to smirk right now; I'm smirking as I write this.)

A few weeks later, my desk is piled high with stacks of papers and I'm wondering why there were so many incomplete assignments when I realize that I've left the Fantasy stage and entered Survival. I'm staring at a workbook for a basal reading series, looking for something to keep my students busy and me sane, when my mentor, Tam Hess, finds me.

"I just saw this flier about a study group about writing instruction. Do you want to go?"

Wild-eyed, I look up from the worksheets. "My students won't write. I have so many incomplete writing assignments; I don't even know what to do."

"I don't know if this study group will help with that," says Tam, "but we get a free book and there'll be snacks. I talked with the principal and he said we can leave school early in order to make it to the study group on time. Do you want to go?"

I look down at my desk and run my fingers across a sticky note on which I'd written a line from Wong's book: *Effective teachers strive for Mastery by reading the literature and going to professional meetings* (7). (I wish I could say it's the drive to reach Mastery that persuades me to say yes, but in reality it's the free book and snacks.)

We're supposed to bring a notebook to the meeting, so I grab one that I bought before school began (Figure 7.1). I look at it and feel like crying. *I wish I were still in Fantasy*, I think.

The quote on the front makes me sigh. There is nothing magical about my classroom. Nothing. It is all I can do to survive each day.

FIGURE 7.1
The first notebook I bought as a teacher. Little did I know this would help transform me into a writer.

The teachers at the meeting are gathered to discuss something called "writing workshop" that they use in their classrooms. It sounds like utopia to me. Teachers deliver a little lesson and then give students time to write. The meeting participants discuss how their students choose their own topics and fill page after page with their own ideas. Participants tell stories about students sharing their writing and entire classes erupting in applause.

I'm skeptical. My students won't even write on the topics I give them. I can't imagine the mass chaos that would ensue if I gave them twenty to thirty minutes to write about anything they wanted. My students hate writing. I know because they tell me. Daily. Loudly. Emphatically.

During the meeting, we are asked to do a quick-write on whatever we want—we just have to write for the entire allotted length of time. No thinking, just writing. "This is a great way to get your students writing because it frees them from the stress of getting it right," says one of the leaders.

I try not to roll my eyes. If I were to try this in my middle school classroom, my students would probably draw all over the pages.

The timer is set and we start writing. I write on a scrap sheet of paper instead of in my notebook; I don't want a record of what I'm feeling. My entire vision of what it means to be a teacher is being shattered. Maybe I completely missed my calling. Maybe I'm doomed to be a failure.

The timer is ticking and everyone around me is writing.

And I remember: *I used to want to be a writer.* Why not write? If I'm going to fail as a teacher, maybe I can at least use the time to learn to be a writer.

I begin putting words on the page. I don't realize that with each letter, each word, each sentence I am stepping out of Survival and becoming a teacher of writers.

The timer goes off and a few people share their writing. Then the people running the meeting give us a book: *Clearing the Way* (1987) by Tom Romano. Between the covers, I meet a teacher-writer who has respect for students and their writing. I learn about writing process in theory and in practice. I realize the power of writing to learn and discover. I find footing for evaluating and grading. The free book gives me the freedom to learn how to meet the needs of the young writers in my classroom.

But I'm still not a believer. After all, Mr. Romano has never set foot in my classroom full of disengaged writers. Mr. Romano's students want to write. Mine want to sleep.

I suddenly decide, *Why not?* Whining and lamenting isn't making a difference. Instead of just taking the bits and pieces from Romano's book and from the meeting, why not take it all? Why not give this workshop deal a whirl? If it flops, I'm only losing one unit of instruction, and besides, it really can't be any worse than what's going on already.

I spend all day Sunday making 125 notebooks by stapling blank copy paper together. (Why should I invest in notebooks when this whole thing is obviously going to fail?) The next day, I pass out the notebooks and have the students decorate their covers.

"You are going to be a mystery writer," I tell them, "and you need a notebook to help you collect ideas for your story. Take some time today to make a cover that will inspire you."

The kids stare at me. I point out the colored pencils and markers and crayons around the room. I direct students to the piles of magazines on the back table and the scissors and glue sticks. I hold up the notebook cover I made late the night before.

"You can't do this wrong," I say. "Just collect some words or pictures that will inspire you to write."

They start moving. Soon there's a buzz in the room as students talk about ideas. It isn't chaos. It isn't loud. B.J. isn't dancing on top of the desks. Students are working with their notebooks and sharing ideas for possible mystery stories.

"Beginner's luck," I tell Mrs. Hess in the hallway after school.

Now that we have notebooks, we have to figure out how to write a mystery. I collect some short mystery stories, provide a quick summary of each one, and leave copies of them in folders on the back table.

"Select one to read and then figure out what makes it a mystery. Then read another." In the name of trusting students as writers, I decide not to be bossy. They can decide what texts to read and how to keep their thoughts to share.

The kids are as engaged as they were while making their notebooks. I pinch myself to make sure I'm not dreaming. My students always avoid reading.

Near the end of workshop, we gather around a piece of chart paper. I write a question at the top of the chart: *What do we need to write a mystery?*

"What did you notice about the mysteries you were reading? What did they have in common?" I ask.

Instead of heads down and dead silence, the students jump into a conversation. We make a list:

Characters

A creepy place

A problem

Lots of people could have done it

"I think we should say 'suspects' for that one," I say. The students nod in agreement. I make the change and ask, "Anything else?" They continue the list:

Talking

Smells and sounds

Clues

An ending that solves the mystery

"I'm thinking about clues," says Jami.

I'm intrigued that even though the list goes on, Jami brings us back to clues. "What about them?" I ask.

"I don't know. Just that . . . well, I guess . . . they didn't always point to the guilty person. They make you think someone else did it."

"Red herrings," Zach says.

Everyone looks to the back corner of the room. I'm not sure what's more shocking: that Zach is awake, that he's talking, or that he's spot-on.

"What are you talking about?" Jami asks.

"Red herrings. That's when there's a clue that makes you think someone else did it. The best mysteries have red herrings so they're not too easy to solve."

As the bell rings, I add "red herrings" to the list.

"It's over already?" I hear someone say as students gather their books. "This class went fast."

It's been another successful day. Once again, I chalk it up to beginner's luck.

As students fill their notebooks, more and more successful days go by. My notebook is filling up, too. It's the only way I can figure out what to teach—I have to do the work as a writer in order to help students write.

I always thought writing a mystery story would be easy. I soon realize that I can add that idea to the growing list of all the things I thought about teaching that would prove to be untrue. I spend hours in my notebook, not only writing, but also trying to figure out what I'm doing as a writer so I can bring it to the classroom.

This is where the tide of mass disengagement turns. When I show students my writing, I have their full attention. When I admit my struggles with figuring out the story, they are willing to try to sort through their own plots. When I register excitement because I figure out how to make action, thinking, and talking work together, it permeates the room and soon most students are trying the same thing.

At the end of the unit, every single student turns in a mystery story—compared to forty-eight percent for the previous writing assignment. Even an English teacher can understand the significance of those statistics!

I claim beginner's luck for the remainder of the year, but the following summer I decide to be intentional about learning to teach writers and start consuming every professional book available about teaching writers. I read Graves and Murray, Atwell and Rief, Ray and Fletcher, Calkins and Anderson. Harry Wong would say I'm on my way toward Mastery.

I soon learn that it isn't beginner's luck enticing my students to write, it's being a teacher who also writes. Of all the things I can do to affect my writing instruction, this is the most important.

In *Radical Reflections* (1993), Mem Fox writes:

> *We know Don Graves has had a profound influence on the teaching of writing. His message has been this: "Look at real writers. Observe their needs. Discover the process they go through and the reasons why they write. Then re-create those conditions in your own classrooms." But we tend not to discover the writing process—we only read about it and imagine that's good enough. It isn't. (35)*

It isn't enough to read about writing. It isn't enough to listen to authors talk about their writing processes. These things are valuable, but they are not enough to entice writers. We must write and discover a process for ourselves. I agree with Mem Fox that writing workshop is a wonderful and flexible idea *and* that it will fail "if we teachers of writing refuse to write ourselves" (40).

When teachers write, we give our students a gift. Suddenly they have a living, breathing writer in the room—someone who understands that writers have rocky days, who knows the difficulty of cutting words during revision, who appreciates the importance of feedback.

When teachers write, we stop creating assignments and begin cultivating a community. Writers thrive when surrounded by people who write. I know this, so I surround myself with writers. I love to talk with writers about writing. I can't believe how different we all are: I write to a word count, but my friend Tam says she'd never do that; I write at home, but my friend Jen writes at Starbucks; I keep a physical notebook full of sketches and lists and maps and notes, but my friend Franki keeps most of her thinking electronically.

As writers, we share common ground. We all find topics to write about and we all work the words. Some of us draft slowly, revising as we go; others plow through a draft, waiting until it is all on paper before we consider revision.

In *How Writers Work* (2000), Ralph Fletcher encourages us to experiment with customizing our writing processes. Personally I find that as I grow and change as a writer, my writing process does as well. Fletcher tells young writers, "Feel free to find your own way of writing, custom-made, a process that works for you. Sometimes you can only find your process through trial and error. If you're like me, your writing process will probably be a messy one" (4).

This advice isn't just for student writers. It's for their teachers, too. When we unlock the writing process for ourselves, we become prepared to guide students as they do the same. This is much more valuable than finding a planning template on Pinterest.

Being a teacher who writes doesn't mean you have to spend hours in your notebook or become a published writer. It simply means writing the same kinds of things you expect your students to write. It means creating stories instead of assignments. I think Lucy Calkins sums it up best in *The Art of Teaching Writing (1994)*:

> *If we ourselves are immersed in an ongoing way in our own writing, we have a fabulous resource to draw from when we teach. But it is not necessary to expect that all of us, as teachers, will regularly draft, revise, and publish our own essays and poems. What is necessary, however, is that we have memories of a time when we loved writing and that we draw on those memories when we teach writing. If we have even once in our lives experienced the power of writing, our teaching will forever be changed. (13)*

When we become teachers who write, our teaching is forever changed and we move into Wong's highest level of teaching—Impact.

CHAPTER 8: WRITING ALWAYS GIVES MORE THAN IT TAKES

n 2013, I went through a period of having trouble finding the motivation to write. For more than five years, I'd established and maintained a daily writing habit. Most days I wrote more than 1,000 words on a writing project. I also wrote blog posts, articles, and notebook entries. I'm an intrinsically motivated writer, but in 2013 I found myself content to clean the house and happy with an earlier bedtime. What happened?

The answer is that we adopted another child. I didn't suddenly lose my energy for writing, but life was changing. We now had four children, and they were beginning to be more involved in extracurricular activities. I had to find my footing as a mom—and in doing so, I started to lose my writing self.

When you don't write regularly, you're more susceptible to believing lies about writing and about yourself as a writer. Maybe I just couldn't make the words work anymore. Maybe my story wasn't worth recording. What if I simply stop writing? Would life be any different? As I contemplated this option, I realized that writing, for me, is essential. In college, preservice teachers learn about intrinsic and extrinsic motivation. I'm not sure about your experience, but in mine, intrinsic motivation was praised and the extrinsic kind scoffed at. Being intrinsically motivated by nature, I found it easy to go along with this and embraced intrinsic motivation over extrinsic both in my personal life and in the classroom.

As a result, I struggled with offering extrinsic motivation to my adopted children. I wanted them to behave because *they* wanted to behave, but many of their behaviors stemmed from their need for attention and survival. By default, their motivation was extrinsic. Lucky for me, my office was next to our school's mental health therapist.

Our paths crossed when I received the cover of *Day by Day,* a book I coauthored with Stacey Shubitz, from Stenhouse. I squealed with delight. On the other side of the wall sat Becca Snider. I couldn't contain myself. I had to show the cover to someone, so I ran next door and squealed again: "Come see the cover of my book!"

Andy and I had recently adopted the girls when Becca and I became friends. She taught me that external motivation was sometimes necessary. I didn't have time, attention, or energy to produce the intrinsic motivation to write with four children, so I decided to consider some external reasons to write. As I began to recognize what writing offers, I found that it gives more than it takes.

WRITING HELPS ME GROW MY THINKING AND MY TEACHING

When I write, I realize new ideas. I make connections. I figure out what I need to do next. When I write about what's happening in classrooms, with colleagues, or in my current reading, something significant happens: I begin to see things from a new perspective. This is how learning happens. This is how growth happens. I stunt myself when I'm not writing. I'm reminded of Rob in the opening chapter of Kate DiCamillo's *The Tiger Rising* (2002):

> *Rob had a way of not-thinking about things. He imagined himself as a suitcase that was too full, like the one that he had packed when they left Jacksonville after the funeral. He made all his feelings go inside the suitcase; he stuffed them in tight and then sat on the suitcase and locked it shut. That was the way he not-thought about things. Sometimes it was hard to keep the suitcase shut. But now he had something to put on top of it. The tiger. (4)*

When I'm not writing, I shove all my not-thinking into a suitcase and sit a tiger on top of it. At first I might feel a little relieved to not-think about how hard it can be to conjure words and even harder to entice students to write. But just as Rob finds in the book, I always find it's hard to keep the suitcase shut. Not-thinking about things doesn't make them go away or allow me to move past the trouble. I have to open the suitcase and face the words head on in order to keep growing. It is only when we, as teachers, face writing ourselves that we are able to entice students to write, too.

WRITING LETS ME SEE THE IMPORTANCE OF MY WORK

Sometimes the daily grind can convince me that the things I'm doing aren't important. A written record of what I do helps me combat these negative thoughts. I'm able to look back and see the truth: Teaching matters. I matter. When I begin doubting myself, it's an indication that I need to put more words on the page. If you ever begin to doubt whether you matter, whether you make a difference, try writing to see that you matter.

Consider the following prompt: *What surprised you recently in your work?* The question invites us to think in specifics and pinpoint a moment that matters. When we write about it, we relive it, tugging at the threads of the memory. Some of the threads pull loose and unravel, but others hold fast when we tug on them, allowing them to weave into the fabric of our lives and create meaningful memories.

Pause for a moment and linger on the prompt and then jot some of your first thoughts. Take time to unfold the memory bit by bit, putting yourself back in the moment.

What surprised you recently in your work?

In her 2006 book Take Joy: A Writer's Guide to Loving the Craft, *Jane Yolen offers the following advice:*

> Be prepared as you write to be surprised by your own writing, surprised
> by what you find out about yourself and about your world. Be ready
> for the happy accident. Open yourself to numinous, to the shapes and
> shades of language, to the first powerful thrust of story, to the character
> that develops away from you (sort of like a wayward adolescent), to the
> surprise of the exact and perfect ending. (5)

Follow the moments that surprise you and you will find out about yourself and your world. You will see that you matter.

WRITING ENERGIZES ME FOR THE DAY

My favorite time to write is very early in the morning, while the rest of the world is asleep. There is something powerful about writing the day into being, placing the importance on collecting words rather than rushing to get out of the door. I also write at night, composing blog posts under a sleeping sky.

Writing fuels me. My neurons start firing and I have new energy for the work ahead of me. Just a few minutes in my notebook and I find renewal.

WRITING MAKES ME SEE MORE ACCURATELY

It is easy to feel overwhelmed as a teacher. If I only rely on my thoughts at any moment, the reality of my work can become distorted. I can begin to believe that teaching is impossible. However, when I put words on the page, the black and white boldness makes me see the possibilities. It renews my belief in the power of our profession and sustains me to keep going.

I love reading and rereading Donald Miller's book, *A Million Miles in a Thousand Years: How I Learned to Live a Better Story* (2009). The book is a celebration of life and shows how to live a meaningful narrative. I think Miller is right when he says, "You don't know a story is happening to you when you're in it. You slide into the flow of it like a current in the ocean; you look back at the beach and can't see your umbrella, and your hotel is a quarter mile behind you" (111). When we write, we capture our stories and make them tangible instead of allowing them to float away in the ocean current. We document them so that we aren't left grasping at the impossible.

WRITING LETS ME TAKE HOLD OF THE SMALL MOMENTS

When writing, it is the tiny details that often hold the most significance. Meaning is built by a pile of tiny details. The same is true in our classrooms: The smallest moments matter most. When I force myself to write, I'm often overwhelmed by the magnitude of it all and intimidated by the blank page. When this happens, I shift to thinking tiny and collect the small moments. In class, I often miss the small moments because I'm so busy scurrying from one thing to the next. Writing makes me slow down and intentionally consider them. These moments turn out to be the sustenance I need to teach well and find meaning in my work.

When I'm not writing, doubts take over and become my reality. I start missing the beauty of kids and the significance of workshop instruction. Writing grounds me and keeps me genuine. It is almost like a magic potion, but of course we know there's much more to it than magic.

The truth is, there is just one thing that keeps teachers from writing. It doesn't take much time, energy, or ability to consistently jot down a few words. It doesn't take brilliance to note the small moments that surprise you or frustrate you or bring you joy. It just takes one thing: dogged resolve. To entice students to write, teachers must write first.

CHAPTER 9: EVERYONE HATES WRITING

Pop quiz time! Which of the following statements have you ever used as a reason not to write?

I don't know what to write.

I don't have a reason to write.

I don't have anything to write about.

I'm not a good writer.

No one reads my writing.

I don't know how to get started.

I don't want to sound dumb.

I'd rather do something else.

I'm too tired.

I don't have time.

I have too many ideas.

I run out of ideas.

I'm not as good as other writers.

I'm not inspired.

I'm not sure what I'm doing.

No one ever comments about my writing.

I'm scared to share my story.

I'm embarrassed about my conventions.

It's only fair that you see the answers I selected:

✓ *I don't know what to write.*

✓ *I don't have a reason to write.*

✓ *I don't have anything to write about.*

✓ *I'm not a good writer.*

✓ *No one reads my writing.*

✓ *I don't know how to get started.*

✓ *I don't want to sound dumb.*

✓ *I'd rather do something else.*

✓ *I'm too tired.*

✓ *I don't have time.*

✓ *I have too many ideas.*

✓ *I run out of ideas.*

✓ *I'm not as good as other writers.*

✓ *I'm not inspired.*

✓ *I'm not sure what I'm doing.*

✓ *No one ever comments about my writing.*

✓ *I'm scared to share my story.*

✓ *I'm embarrassed about my conventions.*

Yes, I've used every single item on the list as a reason why I don't write. I'm a person who wrote her way through childhood and used to dream of becoming a writer. I like to write, often choosing it as a way to spend my free time. Ironically, when I became an English teacher I quit writing (for a bit).

I know all the reasons a person won't write because I used to be that person. On some days, I still am.

It's a misconception to believe that there are writers and nonwriters, that some people can write and others can't.

Everyone can learn to write.

Everyone can put words on the page.

And everyone struggles with wanting to not-write.

Everyone. This is part of living the writing life. As a writer, there are times when you don't want to write—or even worse, when you refuse to. In a whole classroom of writers, there will always be someone who doesn't want to write. The reasons for not wanting to write are varied; often, just as a writer overcomes one of them, another takes hold. This is true for all writers. All writers must overcome not wanting to write.

Merriam-Webster defines *entice* as "to attract or tempt by offering pleasure or advantage." This is the key to helping all students learn to write well. It's not about labeling kids as reluctant or proficient writers. It's not even about experienced or less-experienced writers. Teaching all students to write well is about enticing them to use their words to affect others.

There isn't a single solution to the ancient problem of kids hating to write. Perhaps *hate* doesn't quite capture what many people feel about writing; *loathe, detest, despise,* or *abhor* may be more accurate. I'm married to one of these kinds of people. Andy spent his school career recycling the same book report, research paper, and persuasive essay from sixth grade through twelfth grade. (He even got some mileage out of these assignments in college.) He did turn in different poetry assignments, but only because he plagiarized the latest hit by his favorite heavy metal or alternative band. When forced to write an essay for a test, he complied with the minimal expectations and still did well enough to end up invited to apply for admission at Embry Riddle and MIT.

He continues to complain about writing, even today. He drags his feet writing thank-you notes, whines about filling out paperwork, and crabs about short-answer questions on adoption applications. His friends and family think it is a rich twist of fate that he married an English teacher. They have a dark sense of humor.

In *Content-Area Writing* (2007), Daniels, Zemelman, and Steineke write that teachers "often say that kids hate writing. But maybe what they hate is the kind of writing we make them do" (3). They go on to explain that today's kids are doing more "authoring than any young people in the history of the world" (3).

It is true. Today's kids are connected through social media, sharing their stories in tweets and posts and texts. They are making YouTube videos and interacting through video games and threaded discussions. We are at a time in history when we can use technology for creating original content rather than just consuming other people's ideas. This is why Sir Ken Robinson can assert that "creativity is now as important in education as literacy." I believe creativity and literacy go together like macaroni and cheese.

Andy is always one of my first readers because his response is dependable: "That's good, Ruth." After reading some of this book, he said, "I think I wouldn't hate to write if I were in a writing workshop like you talk about. I could have developed some confidence instead of feeling like I didn't ever know what I was doing." It is necessary to establish solid writing workshops in order to entice students to write and increase their creative thinking.

Andy and I can both agree on one thing: writing is challenging. As humans, we like things easy. So in order to put in the effort and work to learn to write well, we must be enticed. Whether this comes in the form of internal or external motivation doesn't really matter. What matters is that we have a desire to *write*.

CHAPTER 10:
IS WRITING
ESSENTIAL?

Sam writes with me every Saturday morning. It's a longstanding tradition. One day he asked, "May I use your phone? I want to figure out the word for someone who loves words." I handed over the phone and we both learned a new vocabulary word. *Logophile* means "word lover." "That's us," Sam proclaimed. "Writers are logophiles."

Words are enough to entice Sam and me to write on most Saturdays. But even the two of us logophiles need external motivation on some days. A large glass of chocolate milk is motivation for Sam, just like a fresh cup of sweet coffee gets me out of bed earlier on Saturdays than the rest of the week.

Writing makes my life better. I'm better when I write and I'm better when others write and I read their stories. So I wake up early and stay up late to write. It's vital for me, but is it essential for everyone? Do we all have to write to share our stories?

The simple answer is no—no, we do not. Tom Romano shares this brutal truth in *Write What Matters* (2015): "For most people, living a good life and writing are not synonymous" (1). I have to admit that these words sting, but they remain true. Andy doesn't write, and yet I know of no one who lives life better.

Although *writing* isn't essential for a well-lived life, *story* is. If I boil writing down to its bones, what I'm left with is story.

It's not fair to keep story hidden. It's not enough to live it and never share it. Whether we talk or draw or write our stories, the important thing is we share them with people who matter.

We need to share our stories with one another. When we take our stories out, with our hearts pounding and our palms sweaty, we become alive and the world becomes a better place. We understand one another in new ways and we gain grace. Ramona Behnke, author of the blog *Pleasures from the Page*, greets her readers with a quote from Barry Lopez: "Everything is held together by story. That is all that is holding us together. Story and compassion." I'm partial to this idea.

STORY AND COMPASSION

Early in September, I witnessed the way story and compassion hold us together in Cathy Cole's second-grade classroom. Cathy's students were transitioning from an activity into writing workshop. She gave the sign to transition, clicked on some music, and her students began cleaning up and heading to the meeting area.

The music ended and Cathy scanned the class, making sure everyone was ready. She noticed a student and asked, "Gabriel, are you okay?"

Gabriel's eyes were down and he was pulling on a thread of the carpet. His cheeks were blotchy.

Cathy waited.

Gabriel shook his head.

"What's wrong?" asked Cathy.

I was struck by the way Cathy maintained Gabriel's dignity. He wasn't embarrassed, and although the class waited patiently to start the writing lesson, the other students weren't annoyed with the small conversation between student and teacher.

Gabriel's voice was louder than I expected and shook as he spoke.

"You made us stop while I was still messing up. I tried twice and couldn't get the right answer. I needed more time."

Cathy named his emotion. "I feel like that sometimes, too. It's called *frustration*. You are feeling frustrated."

Gabriel nodded and tears spilled out of his eyes. His classmates scooted closer. One rubbed his back, another patted his knee. Cathy said, "Doesn't it feel good to be around a class that understands? They are filling your bucket."

Gabriel nodded. Then Cathy said, "Do you want a hug?" Gabriel wiped his tears with the heel of his hand and nodded. As he stood up, Cathy said, "Everyone, air hug yourself while I hug Gabriel." She hugged Gabriel and everyone else gave themselves an air hug.

I blinked back tears as Cathy started the lesson. The entire exchange took less than two minutes.

This is the role of today's teacher. It is not enough to know content. It is not enough to be kind and empathetic. We must be both.

Cathy's minilesson that day was a turning point in the class's unit, but her instruction didn't suffer because she displayed empathy. In fact, it was enhanced. Here's how she introduced the minilesson:

"Today we are thinking about times to write about. I read your stories last night and they kind of made me fall asleep."

Cathy mimed a giant yawn and her students giggled. "You guys! I kept thinking, I know they have more interesting stories to tell. Today let's think of different times to write about. "Like Gabriel was feeling frustrated. Does anyone else have a time when they felt frustrated?"

The second graders thought and soon thumbs started popping up—a sign of ideas brewing in Cathy's classroom. Stories started flying as students shared with their writing partners without Cathy's direction.

Gabriel wasn't alone. Almost everyone was sharing about a frustrated time. This is the power of story. It changes lives by teaching us

- *to connect to others and find we're more alike than different,*
- *to own the story we are living, and*
- *to believe we can keep rewriting the next part of our story.*

For these reasons, writing workshop is essential to education. Not because every child should grow up to be a writer, but because we all must learn to communicate our stories, our beliefs, our knowledge in order to make the world a better place.

CHAPTER 11:
WRITING WORKSHOP
IS ESSENTIAL

Many children are authoring their own texts before they ever set foot in a school building. This is true for my son Sam. He produced a digital story, *Train Parts*, before he was five. When he was a second grader, he started a blog (complete with a Lego avatar). He knows how to send e-mail, create shared Google Drive documents, post to Instagram and Twitter, engage in Facebook feeds (using his personal hashtag, #hijackedbysam), comment on blog posts, and upload videos to YouTube. He manages Netflix lists, creates Amazon wish lists (with priority levels), and, starting in fourth grade, designs and orders our Christmas cards. Sam even found a pen pal through reading and commenting on Deb Day's blog, *Coffee with Chloe*. Sam and Deb's dog Chloe have been e-mailing and swapping gifts for years.

For Sam and many of his peers, writing doesn't just mean putting pencil to paper. It is creating movies and collaborating with other people online. It is social media and staging photos to convey an important message. No longer should we consider writing an isolated activity. Writing is the creation of a project that uses text, image, sound, and other media to share a message. The definition of *to write* is a wide-open frontier for today's students to explore.

Writing workshop is a hub for innovation and creation. It was designed to empower students to make choices as writers in order to create meaningful writing projects while learning the craft of writing. Even though the concept has been around for many years, it can expand to meet the demands of today's students.

Writing is writing. It doesn't matter if it is done with pencil and paper, typed on a keyboard, or recorded into a phone. We don't need to differentiate between digital writing and paper writing. I don't consider myself a paper-pencil writer or a digital writer; I'm simply a writer who uses a variety of tools.

Sometimes I post a picture and a caption on Instagram as a way to hold an idea or pull at a thread, much like I do in my writing notebook. For example, I posted the picture and caption shown in Figure 11.1. Maggie Roberts left a comment on my random thoughts that made me think more deeply. The next day, when I was out running with my kids, I was pondering Maggie's comments when Sam turned around to help Steph, who was struggling to keep pace with us. He reached over and took her hand. I snapped a picture.

Later that night I wrote an entry in my notebook, tugging on the thread Maggie said was worthy.

When I'm trying to figure out what I believe, I open a blog-post window and type a flash draft of my thoughts. I use Twitter as a holding tank for articles and quotes. I write leads to articles by hand after listening to podcasts about science, technology, and history. Then I frantically type drafts on my laptop before the ideas bolt from my brain.

My writing process is changing with access to new tools, and the same goes for our students. More classrooms are filled with more devices than ever before. Schools are spending millions of dollars to connect their students to technology. There are gimmicks and programs offering empty promises of better writers. App stores are filled with quick fixes and "guaranteed" motivational strategies for student writers. Some apps and websites do empower writers in remarkable new ways, offering students access to resources they could never tap before, but the continuum is vast and there is a chasm separating the quality of resources.

As we explore and expand the resources students can use as writers, there is potential for both good and harm. Take e-mail as an example. Hannah and Sam both have access to e-mail. Hannah used it for harm, sending more than four e-mails per minute in English class, stirring drama and inviting harsh consequences. Sam used it for good, connecting with a pen pal to talk books, research, and writing.

FIGURE II.I
Using digital platforms as a tool for writing

START WITH WHY

When I first learned to teach writers, it didn't take me long to exhaust all the scripted lessons I had for writing workshop. After teaching the two from *Writing Workshop: The Essential Guide* by Ralph Fletcher and JoAnn Portalupi (2001), I had to figure out what students needed so I could know what to teach next.

I couldn't buy the answer with a pretty PDF back then. Blog posts with cute printables didn't exist, nor did YouTube lessons. Today, of course, instructional resources are abundant. I once heard a teacher describe lesson planning these days as a buffet table, filled with so many choices it's easy to get overwhelmed. But just because something is available doesn't mean it is good for you.

In earlier years, I had to put in the time to *think and think and think* and figure out what my students needed as writers. I filled notebooks trying to sort out my thoughts. Sometimes I wonder what it would have been like if I'd had access then to all the resources available today. Would it have made teaching writers easier? Would I have honed the art of teaching students to write? Back then, I learned to figure out what students needed by

- *writing alongside them,*
- *reading them mentor texts, and*
- *conferring with them.*

If I'd had the resources back then that we have today, I wonder if I would have had a false sense of security. I wonder if I would have depended on the resources for direction, rather than learning to follow the students in my classroom. I would have had everything students needed to perform as writers without laying the foundation for why they should do so.

My instruction would have been much tidier and streamlined, but it wouldn't have been as mindful. When I did the work to discern how writers learn, being led by vetted and research-based professional books and journal articles, I discovered the truth about how to teach writers. I learned how to apply best practices in meaningful and authentic ways, without blindly choosing whatever was immediately attractive and easily available.

At the same time, I know that many resources can lift the level of writing workshop instruction. I've seen instruction transform as teachers use video minilessons and make adjustments to future lessons by assessing what's effective and what isn't. I've also seen instruction transform when teachers have a conference note system established and a guide for questions to ask in a conference.

When was the last time you listed your core beliefs? This is a practice I engage in often. Because things are changing so rapidly for educators, I've found it essential to regularly check my core beliefs. Won't you join me? Take some time to consider these questions:

· *Why is writing workshop an essential part of the school day?*

· *Why is it important for students to share their stories?*

· *What do I believe about how children learn to write?*

Keep this list handy throughout the school year and check to make sure your practice is aligned with your beliefs. If I believe students ought to have time to share their writing, but I always run out of time for sharing, then my actions don't reflect my core beliefs. Unless I'm intentional about aligning my actions to my core beliefs, it's easy to get off course. When I recognize that my actions don't mirror my beliefs, I make changes. For example, I might start writing workshop with a share session. This way, sharing happens before we run out of time.

When we are given the *how* to teach without knowing the *why* that supports it, then writing workshop becomes a precarious strategy. If we are going to fight for its essential role in school, then we need to know what we believe about teaching students to write.

It takes wherewithal to ensure that every student grows as a writer. Even with the plethora of resources available to us, it takes time and tenacity to develop the art of workshop instruction. Many classrooms are replete with stress, making it difficult for teachers to learn the craft of workshopping. Unfortunately, this stress leads to the writing workshop struggling to survive.

It would be easier not to mention this predicament. After all, the main point of this chapter is to emphasize that writing workshop is essential for today's students. There is power in knowing how to write well and in being able to communicate through narrative, informative, and argumentative writing. Every child deserves the opportunity to learn how to craft words and work conventions in order to influence others. Writing workshop is the best vehicle for students to become the kind of people who are positive world changers. (Cue the rainbows and butterflies.)

Teachers are always looking for ways to meet the demands and expectations placed on our overstuffed curricula, standards that leave child development in the dust, and schedules that work on paper but not in reality. Knowing our core beliefs about teaching writers is critical to successfully meeting these demands.

We must make sacrifices to protect writing workshop. First, we must battle for the minutes. Then, we must get comfortable living in the mess that comes with growing writers. Finally, we must learn to figure things out so that our writing instruction becomes top-notch.

YES, WRITING WORKSHOP IS ESSENTIAL

Students have untapped stories and messages locked inside their hearts. Some kids don't even know they have worthy stories. They're simply trying to survive rather than thrive. Other kids haven't realized the power of their voices. They don't know they can share messages with the world.

More than ever, it is essential for us to be savvy communicators. Writing workshop allows all kids, not just the affluent or gifted, an opportunity to be strong writers. If we remove writing workshop from classrooms, the risk is grave. Students will not become solid communicators, and our world will suffer from the lack of their voices.

CHAPTER 12:
DEVELOPING
FAITHFUL AND
FEARLESS WRITERS

A t dinner, Stephanie retells a conversation with her language arts teacher.

"I asked why I have to write about such a stupid topic for my persuasive essay. I said I wanted to choose my topic, not write about something stupid that I don't know about and is complicated to find out about."

"Did you really use the word stupid with your teacher?" I ask, trying not to match her indignation. She has a point, though: How does the teacher know what Stephanie is passionate enough to write about with conviction for a persuasive essay?

Stephanie nods. "Twice, but only because I used self-control. I wanted to say 'stupid, stupid, stupid.' Anyway, she told me she wanted to challenge us, that's why we have to write about a stupid topic."

"She thinks the topic is stupid?"

"I don't know. I asked her, 'Wouldn't it be better to let us pick a topic so we could actually learn how to write a stupid essay?'"

"I bet that went over well," I say.

"Not really," Stephanie says. "She just said, 'You're in your argument mode so I'm not talking to you about this anymore.' So I still have to fill out this stupid worksheet about a stupid topic and tonight I have to find a stupid quote and she said I should talk to you, Mom."

I raise my eyebrows. "Did you tell her I helped you last night?"

"No way! She thinks you're actually a good writer or something," Steph assures me in her twelve-year-old way. "I don't want her to know you really don't know what you're doing either!"

Stephanie's teacher is a passionate educator. She cares deeply for her students and she wants them to grow as readers and writers. Like many teachers, she's also looking for a way to add challenge and rigor to her classroom.

I have a hard time with a word that in its original Latin means *stiffness*, and today serves as a shortened version of *rigor mortis*, or death. Do we really want rigor to define our classrooms? I know that Stephanie's teacher, like us, does not want stiffness and death to define her assignments.

Sometimes, in our pursuit to increase the challenge of our writing projects, we end up with stiff assignments that annihilate young writers' passion. Instead of conniving students into writing, I suggest we learn to entice them. If we trace the roots of the word *entice* back to its Latin origins, we find it meant "firebrand," which then became an Old French word meaning "to set on fire."

Yes, I would rather set students' passion on fire to write than create stiff and lifeless writers. Today, *entice* means to incite or provoke. I must ask myself: What kind of writers do I want to incite?

My first response is that I want to entice joyful writers. Then I think a little more and realize that *I'm* not always a joyful writer. Sometimes I'm a mad writer or a sad writer or an annoyed writer. There are times I write not for the joy of writing, but for the pleasure of having written. This is a common claim among writers. Credit for the statement "I don't like to write, but like having written" is difficult to find, but can be traced back to Frank Norris in 1915. Since then, many other writers have shared this sentiment, often changing the word *like* to *love*.

Joy doesn't always entice writers. Although I did decide a long time ago to be a joyful writer, so there is some element of joy that does incite me to write. It certainly doesn't incite Stephanie; writing is at the bottom of a long list of activities that bring joy to her. I'm sure she's not alone. There are many children sitting in writing workshops who do not find writing to be joyful.

FAITHFUL AND FEARLESS WRITERS

When we entice writers, I suggest we help them to become faithful and fearless writers. The world needs stronger stories. We're here to live a story and we're made to live a good one.

FAITHFUL WRITERS

Writing is creation, and creation is messy. It's not a lockstep process. It's not a guarantee. Most of our best work is completely unexpected. This is why we must be faithful writers: Showing up day after day is the best way to ensure success.

The most important quality I possess as a writer is that *I keep showing up to write*. Even when I don't want to, even when it's become rote, even when the whole rest of my world is falling apart, I'm sure that I can still place words on the page and find meaning.

I need to write to find meaning. Right now, for instance, I'm shooting in the dark. I'm not quite sure how this chapter is going to take shape. One of the kids is pounding on my door and I'm doing my best to ignore the rhythmic beating and the "MOM!" squawked on every fourth beat.

I believe it's a myth that we need certain conditions to write. Yes, conditions help. Right now I might be better positioned to write well if I were at Starbucks instead of listening to a bedtime fit. Thankfully, the tantrum is short-lived: There is now silence outside my door and the words are still stacking up on the page.

No, we don't need perfect conditions to write. What we need is faith.

The writers in our classrooms need to learn faith. Even under ideal conditions, a whole slew of reasons can keep students from writing. Forgotten notebooks, fights with friends, fire drills, headaches, a book they just have to finish, trouble spelling a word, the upcoming football game: All of these things and more have the potential to derail writers.

One thing keeps us going: *faith*. When writers believe their words matter, nothing can stop them.

Dillon refused to write when I first met him in Christi Overman's second-grade classroom. Things were rough for Dillon, and writing was no exception. Slowly, through illustration, he started putting his stories on paper. His other teachers and I would continue to nudge Dillon as a writer. By the end of the school year, he developed a fluent process and could write with meaning and conventions.

Dillon learned to be a faithful writer because he was given time and space to write daily. We wrapped strong arms around him, supporting him as he learned to find his footing as a writer.

I work across grade levels, and it's been a privilege to watch Dillon grow older. He wasn't always in classrooms with consistent writing workshops, and early on developed a reputation as a non-writer. His teachers lamented that he was lazy and bullheaded when it came to writing.

Dillon would often find me in the hallway before school. He would pull a tattered composition book out of his backpack and show me his latest project: a graphic novel. He went through notebook after notebook after notebook, yet refused to write in the classroom.

In middle school, someone bumps into Dillon outside my office, sending his books flying across the hallway. I stoop down to help him gather them. When I picked up the tattered composition book, I pause.

"You're still writing?" I ask.

"Not really," he says. He pushes his hair out of his eyes.

"Do you mind if I look inside?" I ask.

He shrugs. "I guess."

I open the notebook to find page after page filled with tiny print. Words jumbled across each line. It's not easy to read, but it's bulging with stories.

"You're a writer," I tell him.

"Don't tell anyone," he says, taking the notebook from me.

"Why not?" I ask.

"It's not the kind of writing they want me to do."

"Why do you write?"

He shrugs, slides his composition book between two books, and tucks the stack under his arm. I don't think he's going to answer me, but he does. His voice is quiet and I strain to hear him.

"I guess I just couldn't stop after we wrote every day in second grade."

I watch the faithful writer walk away.

FEARLESS WRITERS

As we guide students to rewrite their stories of hard into hope, we help them to become fearless writers who are confident that their messages matter. When we help brains heal, we position students to have the confidence they need to write fearlessly.

Arielle was a student in Dan Gause's fifth-grade class. Her dad passed away early in the school year, and she was offered invitations to write all year. For this, she kept a writing notebook. In writing workshop, Mr. Gause taught students to write across genres, topics, audiences, and purposes. Arielle had plenty of space to write about things that mattered.

In the spring, Arielle brought a folded piece of paper to Mr. Gause. It was a poem about her dad.

Arielle had become a fearless writer.

Ralph Fletcher (2002) teaches us that poetry is an ideal container to write about the things that mean the most, and I think he's right, but it took more than knowing about the genre for Arielle to be a fearless writer. Mr. Gause set the stage to entice Arielle and to give her the confidence to write a brave poem.

Writers develop confidence when they learn to believe in themselves *as* writers. Often, the most successful people are not the best at what they do, but the ones with the confidence and perseverance to reach their goals.

GET READY TO LEAP!

When students are faithful and fearless writers, they find the joy in having written. Students become faithful and fearless when they have teachers who are themselves faithful and fearless in their instruction. It's time to take some leaps of faith to establish essential writing workshops that build faithful and fearless writers.

PART III

MOVES TO ENTICE STUDENTS TO WRITE

CHAPTER 13:
LEAPS OF FAITH

My grandparents live in a valley in the Ozarks. To get to their home, you must wind around the mountain on a narrow red clay road. At the base of the mountain there's a creek to drive through. The water rushes under a slab of cement that you slowly drive over. If it rains and the creek rises, you're stuck in the valley until the water level falls.

Whenever we visited, my brother and I played by the creek. There were large rocks scattered across the creek that were perfect as landing pods as we jumped, jumped, jumped, to the far bank. If we could figure out a way across, then we could visit Uncle Bryan and his horses on the other side.

It always looked so easy when Uncle Bryan or Dad jumped across. I would stand on the first rock, my purple gym shoes perfectly positioned to launch me to the next rock. The first few rocks weren't so bad because they were wide, flat, and close together. In the middle of the creek, things changed. The water rushed a little faster out there, making the rocks wetter. Wet rocks make slick rocks. The rocks were also smaller, making it harder to hit the target when you jumped. Plus they were spaced farther apart, making the distance to jump longer.

Recently I returned to the valley with my kids. I took them to the creek to jump from rock to rock to rock. I found myself stuck halfway across. I knew where I wanted to be—the other side of the creek—but I found that the only way to get there was a leap of faith.

Sometimes I feel the same way working with student writers. We are where we are, a community of writers who write together and celebrate together. I know it is only a matter of time before the honeymoon wears off, the endorphins from the creative work disperse, and the thrill of being a writer is no longer so dreamy. We stand on a rock and look to where we want to be. We want to be faithful writers who have the wherewithal to write day after day and who believe in the writing process because we've been through it enough times to trust that it works. The way to empower students to become these kinds of writers is to take leaps of faith.

There is an art to enticing writers. We mustn't gush or sugar-coat things. At the same time, there's no need to throw a bucket of cold water on writers either. We're looking for a place in the middle that will both challenge and cheer students to keep writing.

Following is a collection of stepping stones for making leaps of faith to entice all students to write. Begin with "Cultivate a Celebration Mindset." This is a first leap and it is essential. Then browse the other sections and select one that calls to you.

Just like crossing the creek in the heart of the Ozarks, there isn't only one path. We can each select different leaps. The important thing is that we take the first step and then keep going.

These leaps are not intended to be taken all at once. Plan to linger. Each leap includes the why and then works through the how by identifying moves to make. The moves are connected to the kids they will help. If one of your students is struggling with a specific issue, like low confidence or stamina, then you can find moves tailored to your situation. You will find a pairing of reflection and practical steps for each leap. This is because teaching writers is often more about a stance than a strategy.

As Henry David Thoreau wrote, "We must walk consciously only part way toward our goal, and then leap in the dark to our success." It's time to take leaps of faith toward enticing students to be faithful and fearless writers.

The following table outlines the leaps and moves we can make to entice students to write.

LEAP	NO.	MOVE TO MAKE	KIDS IT HELPS
Chapter 14: Cultivate a Celebration Mindset	1	Notice what students are almost doing as writers.	Students who have low confidence in themselves as writers
	2	Name the small improvements students make toward becoming conventional writers.	Students who are stifled by perfectionism and are easily frustrated with mistakes
	3	Move from trying to fix errors to seeing them as opportunities for growth.	
Chapter 15: Individualizing the Writing Process	4	Show kids a path through a writing project.	Students who are easily confused by or get lost in the writing process
	5	Build curiosity.	Students who don't want to keep a writer's notebook Students who don't have anything to write about
	6	Make a plan.	Students who are disorganized and don't know what to do next
	7	Write a draft in a way that works for you.	Students who freeze when it's time to write a first draft
	8	Celebrate a finished draft and prepare to write another.	Students who write one draft and claim to be done
	9	Establish a Selection Day.	Students who never finish a draft
	10	Model revision with your own writing in front of students.	Students who write one draft and claim to be done
	11	Provide students with tools to encourage revision.	
	12	Make revision simple and satisfying.	
	13	Stand up for imperfect student use of conventions.	Students who are stifled by perfectionism and are easily frustrated with mistakes
	14	Teach students to be effective peer editors.	Students who write one draft and claim to be done
	15	Host a formal writing celebration.	Students who are motivated by external factors
Chapter 16: Writing Projects That Make You Want to Write	16	Offer choice in writing projects.	Students who have little or no stamina or motivation as writers
	17	Convince students there is an audience that cares about reading their writing.	
	18	Validate student topic ideas.	
	19	Build genre knowledge.	
	20	Find personal reasons to write.	

LEAP	NO.	MOVE TO MAKE	KIDS IT HELPS
Chapter 17: Stretch Mentors to Meet Needs	21	Stretch mentors for a variety of inspiration.	Students who have low confidence in themselves as writers
	22	Support students in finding and claiming a writing mentor.	Students who have little or no stamina or motivation as writers
	23	Focus on a small part of the mentor text.	
	24	Research favorite writers to learn more about them as mentors.	
	25	Introduce students to poets as mentors.	
Chapter 18: Simplify Conferring	26	Name the strengths students have as writers.	Students whose writing is difficult to read or understand
	27	Be intentional to teach one main point in every conference.	Students who are motivated by external factors
	28	Offer a measurable challenge for trying out the teaching point.	Students who like a challenge
	29	Increase students' energy levels for writing by listening with empathy.	Students who need to feel connected
	30	Increase students' energy for writing by asking open-ended questions while conferring.	Students who have a difficult time talking about their writing or writing process
	31	Develop the habit of checking back with students after a conference.	Students who need accountability
Chapter 19: Expand Feedback Beyond the Teacher	32	Diversify the end of workshop share sessions to provide more opportunities for students to share and hear about their writing.	Students who are reluctant to believe adults
	33	Offer feedback that will both cheer and challenge writers.	Students who are motivated by external factors
	34	Provide time for students to share the mental battle of being a writer.	
	35	Use writing notebooks to collect written feedback.	
Chapter 20: Tap Technology	36	Select technology tools and apps that support the core beliefs of writing workshop.	Students who want to make an impact or connect beyond the walls of the classroom
	37	Leverage social media to entice students to write.	Students who like to connect (or want to connect) on social media

CHAPTER 14:
CULTIVATE A
CELEBRATION
MINDSET

J ay is a repulsive dinner companion. He eats with his hands, uses his lips as scoop shovels around the edge of his plate, stands up, crawls under the table, stands on his chair, slurps, chews with his mouth wide open and sprays food on anyone who is in the way as he talks while he chews. He had to move to Andy's end of the table when things became too gross for me to handle.

At the same time, Jay is one of the most grateful dinner companions I have ever known. He loves food and appreciates good food. He is always the first to say thank you for the meal. He enjoys trying new food and loves unique combinations. He is excited with each bite and constantly compliments the chef. He engages in conversations, has a quick wit, and listens to others. His ear-to-ear smile while he eats is enough to melt any heart.

Regardless of the gratitude, Jay needs to develop table manners. (A compliment is always easier to accept when it isn't coupled with chunks of food spit across the table.) At first, we tried reminders. The problem was there were so many issues that the entire dinner conversation was about correcting Jay. The girls were grossed out too, so they chimed in with their own snarky reminders. Sam refused to hold Jordan's hand during grace and eventually refused to sit across from him because Jordan's half-chewed food kept landing on his plate.

Jordan's manners did not improve and the enjoyment of dinner plummeted for everyone. We needed a new approach, so we turned to praise.

Instead of saying, "Stop chewing with your mouth open!" we would say, "It looks like you are really enjoying your taco. Will you keep your lips together while you chew?" Jay would smile and seal his lips.

Instead of saying, "Quit eating with your hands!" we would say, "Thanks for setting the table. You put all of the silverware in the correct places, so it'll be easy to use." Jay would smile and pick up his fork.

Instead of saying, "Don't put your lips on the table. They aren't a shovel!" we would say, "Since you enjoy your food so much, if you take smaller bites it will last longer." Jay would smile and close the scoop shovel.

Jordan's table manners continue to improve. When I consider the progress I've made in life, I can often trace a line back to specific praise I received. Praise precedes progress. The same is true for kids.

THE CELEBRATION MINDSET

Instead of focusing on the things students don't do well, consider the things they are *almost* doing as writers. As they begin to improve, celebrate the small victories. Student writing will never be perfect, and I'm grateful for this truth. It shouldn't be perfect. Five-year-old writers ought to create writing that looks like it was written by a five-year-old. Inventive spelling, misplaced capital letters, and crooked letter formation are to be expected. By the same token, I expect adolescents to produce sentence fragments due to subordinate clauses that stand alone. Writing is a reflection of the writer, and our students are learning and growing in all kinds of ways. Because they are developing as writers, they will inevitably produce errors.

Primary-grade writers love the power of ending punctuation. When young writers learn to use this writing feature, they often start using it all over the place. There might be a period after every word or an exclamation point at the end of every line.

This isn't something to get upset about. It is evidence of learning. When ending punctuation begins showing up all over, rather than wondering why students don't know how to use it, consider what they *do* know. If periods are *at the end* of each word, or exclamation points are *at the end* of each line, or question marks are *at the end* of the page, these students know a very important truth about ending punctuation: It goes *at the end* of something. They are *almost* using ending punctuation conventionally.

Move to Make No. 1: Notice what students are *almost* doing as writers.

When older writers are learning to develop a scholarly voice, they often overuse quotations and neglect to attribute them. When faced with an essay filled with such quotations, we can still find something to celebrate.

"I see you are using your scholarly voice by including quotations from experts in the field," we might say, followed by a pause and a smile. More than likely, the student will smile and feel good about the choice to include expert quotes. And, in fact, they are *almost* using expert quotes in a way that develops a solid scholarly voice.

We might continue: "One of the reasons a quote helps to strengthen your scholarly voice is because you are adding the voice of an expert from the field. In order for the reader to know the importance of the quote, you should include an attribution. Let me show you how to do this."

The conversation then shifts as you teach the student how to add an attribution. There is much to learn in becoming a writer, and it is unrealistic for us to expect students to execute everything perfectly.

Move to Make No. 2: Name the small improvements students make toward becoming conventional writers.

Celebration lives alongside the messiness of learning; we simply must learn how to see it. We see and accept the mess when young toddlers are learning to eat. The same mindset is powerful when teaching writers: We don't want to avoid the mess; we want to find joy in the learning. Rather than seeking to eradicate every mistake, let's use mistakes to see what students already know. We can look for signs of learning instead of getting stuck in the mess. We find the things students *almost* know as writers and then we help them improve. Shifting from trying to fix errors to asking, "How is this error evidence of learning?" is how we cultivate a celebration mindset.

Move to Make No. 3: Move from trying to fix errors to seeing them as opportunities for growth.

Errors are not the enemy. In fact, they help us out by pointing to students' needs as writers. It's fairly obvious what a student needs to know as a writer when there's a period after each word. As students become more experienced writers, sometimes the errors aren't always so glaring.

I've argued with myself about using the word *error* here. I'm afraid you will only think about conventions. Conventions are important to writers, but so is process and craft. I often ask myself when reviewing student work, "What is the writer doing, and how can I help him or her do it better?"

When I see Jeffrey with eight sticky notes chained to his draft, I want to shout, "Stop wasting sticky notes!" However, if I stop myself and ask, "What is this writer doing?" I recognize a revision technique that relies on sticky notes. Jeffrey is revising! This is noteworthy and worthy of celebrating.

Then I ask the second half of the question: "How can I help Jeffrey do it better?" Since the sticky notes are all blank, I clearly need to nudge Jeffrey to do some writing. I also notice that his draft is only four lines long. Jeffrey can add to the end of his draft instead of creating a chain of sticky notes.

When I pause and ask, "What is this writer doing, and how can I help him do it better?" I am able to engage my celebration mindset. Thankfully this is something everyone can hone.

TAKING THE FIRST STEPS

Ask yourself the following questions to start cultivating a celebration mindset with your students:

- *What are three things you would want to change about what your students do as writers? Perhaps you wish they would write longer. Maybe you're tired of the endless cries of "I have nothing to write about." If only your students used the correct form of* there *(or* they're, *or* their). *Maybe you wish they would peer-edit more effectively (or even at all). Write down your three biggest pet peeves.*

- *Now, flip these pet peeves to find the celebration they point to. Help students develop stamina by taking a class word count or setting a timer. Are they writing more today than they did yesterday? Maybe they don't know what to write about, but they are really good at telling stories or having all of their supplies with them. Perhaps they know the procedure for peer-editing and offering kind feedback, but need to learn how to offer constructive feedback. Ask yourself how you can help your students do these things better.*

- *Publicly acknowledge what your students are doing well as writers, perhaps at the end of writing workshop during the share session. You could also share what students are doing well as writers via bulletin board, weekly newsletter, Facebook page, or Twitter feed. Remember: praise precedes progress.*

CHAPTER 15:
INDIVIDUALIZING THE
WRITING PROCESS

The writing process can feel overwhelming to long-time professional writers. Just because a writer has written a successful book or is an award-winning journalist doesn't make the writing process easy. I always keep this in mind when working with student writers.

I've seen lots of children stop writing because of the series of hoops they must jump through in the name of the writing process. I've also seen many children turned off by having to write to the specifics of an assignment. When teachers understand that there are two approaches to teaching writers—the product approach and the process approach—we can better tailor our writing instruction to entice students to write.

The product approach focuses on *producing* writing and is typified by a series of assignments that every student must produce. Sometimes these assignments include the same first sentences or transition sentences. By contrast, the process approach focuses on *the process of creating* writing. Students in process-approach classrooms can go months or even the entire year without completing a product. Early in my career, I determined that I fell on the process approach side of the fence. (See Figure 15.1 for a breakdown of differences between the two approaches to writing instruction.)

FIGURE 15.1
The differences between product and process approaches to teaching writers

PRODUCT APPROACH	PROCESS APPROACH
Mentor texts used to imitate	*Mentor texts to inspire original ideas*
Organization of ideas valued	*New and unique ideas valued*
One draft	*Several drafts*
Isolated	*Collaborative*
Emphasis on product	*Emphasis on creative process*

I often remind myself that a writer has a process *in order to produce a product.* I no longer see the two approaches as mutually exclusive. I don't feel like I'm on one side of the fence. Today, I sit on the fence, holding open a gate between the two approaches. (See Figure 15.2.)

FIGURE 15.2
Both product and process approaches are necessary to teaching students to write.

WRITERS. . .
use mentor texts for inspiration and imitation.
develop new ideas as they work on a project.
develop an organized structure for the writing project.
write one draft for a project; write several drafts for a project.
work alone. Work collaboratively.
emphasize the final project and the creative process.

If we focus solely on product, then we don't develop capable and confident writers, just students who may (or may not) write for a grade. Students often feel pressure to produce perfection—to ensure that every word is spelled correctly or that there are five paragraphs, each with three to five sentences. It is difficult to entice students to write (especially students who don't care about grades) when we focus solely on the product.

Of course, if we focus only on the *process,* we can also do students a disservice. Students can get lost sketching in their notebooks. They might write a new draft every day, but never complete one. They might make meaningless plans or no plans at all or spend forever filling out a graphic organizer. They might revise using highlighters and take turns working as peer editors. A month or two can pass without these students growing at all as writers. Yikes!

See why I sit on the fence? It is here I can help students become capable and confident writers. They learn to make the writing process work for them so they can produce high-quality writing projects that are pleasing to both the writer and the reader.

Move to Make No. 4: Show kids a path through a writing project.

This is where a writing process chart comes in handy. Students must learn to trust the writing process. Sometimes we make this more complicated than it needs to be. Any child who can put words or illustrations on the page has a writing process. Once I realized this, I was able to approach individualizing the writing process by honoring the strategies students already had in place.

When I share my writing process chart, I start with a disclaimer. All writers have a process, but rarely do we find two writers who have exactly the same one. And yet, we do find there are a few common phases almost all writers work through in order to prepare their writing projects for an audience.

The writing process is both simple and complex. There are only a handful of steps, but as many ways to execute each one as there are writers on the globe. This truth makes it tricky to balance both the steps of the writing process and the needs of individual writers. Inevitably, there are some writers in the room who have a writing plan done in sixty seconds and others who can't finish one after sixty minutes. Some students can crank out a draft in one day; others need

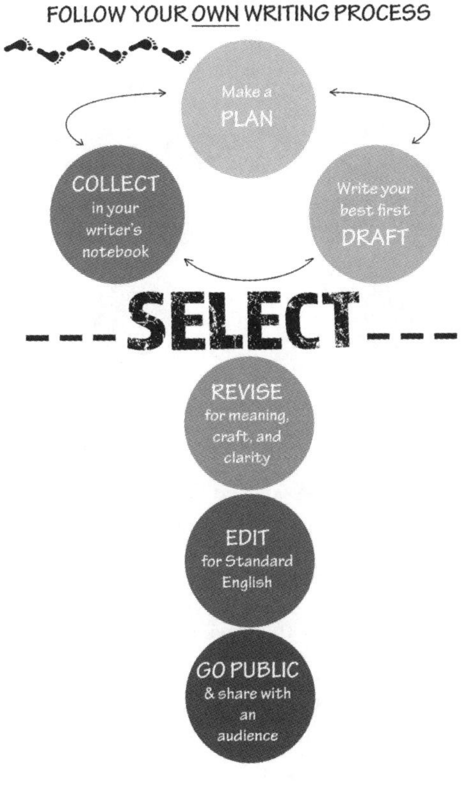

FIGURE 15.3
Writing process chart for older writers

FIGURE 15.4
Writing process chart for younger writers

several. Some writers form a complete plan; others draft a little, then plan a little. It is easy to become overwhelmed by the diversity of the writers in a classroom.

The more I write, the more I realize I don't always develop a plan first. Nor do I revise everything I draft. My notebook is a tool I use throughout the process, not only during "prewriting." The more I considered the ways I expected students to work through the writing process in writing workshop, the more I realized many of my expectations contradicted what I myself do as a writer. My writing process is not lockstep. I do not march through each step and neatly develop a perfect piece of writing. Those who say otherwise are either selling something or teaching writing without writing themselves. It's unfair to send students the message that writing works in such an orderly fashion.

Over several years, I began to adjust the traditional writing process chart to more accurately represent what I knew of my own writing process and of students working as writers. Figures 15.3 and 15.4 show the writing process charts I reimagined and now depend on to help students find and refine their own individual writing processes.

COLLECTING

To begin, I changed the way I talked about prewriting. This term was confusing to me. Did it mean to make a plan? Or was it more about jotting down ideas? Was sketching prewriting? And what if I needed to jot down a list while I was in the middle of my draft? Was this also prewriting even though I already started writing? What about the stuff I wrote in my notebook that wasn't really for a project, but that I wanted to keep in case I ever needed it? Was *this* prewriting? I found students struggled with the term as well. For kids like Stephanie who think writing is "stupid, stupid, stupid," unclear terms do not help.

So, I changed the name to *collecting*.

Writers collect. They collect random inspiration—things they notice and conversations they overhear. They collect around a single idea when beginning a project. They also collect possibilities for revision. They collect ideas for future projects. And they collect bits and pieces of life that may (or may not) have significance. Collection can happen throughout the writing process and encompasses more than just the ambiguous idea of prewriting. (See Figure 15.5.)

Things to COLLECT:

Quick Writes
Lists
Webs
Sketches
Research Notes
Questions & Wonderings
Plans
Revised Leads & Endings
Poetry
Maps

Photos
Notes
Cards
Wrappers
Tags
Ticket Stubs
Poetry
Song Lyrics
Magazine Clippings

FIGURE 15.5
Create a chart with students about things they can collect in their writing notebooks.

FIGURE 15.6
Working in my notebooks gives me energy.

Once I share with students that a notebook is like a junk drawer for their lives, they usually come up with an abundance of ideas for things they can add to their notebooks. Their creative juices kick in and soon our chart is filled with ideas of things and ways to collect them in notebooks. Their notebooks begin to come alive.

For many students, this "junk drawer" becomes a magical storehouse of ideas for writing. But this isn't true for every student. It seems as though students with the roughest histories either love or hate their notebooks. For some, they are safe havens; for others, they are just more obstructions in the way of getting meaningful writing done.

Different writers spend different amounts of time in each phase of the writing process. Since I tend to be an elaborate collector, many of the students I work alongside are, too. But it's just as okay for students to use their notebooks in minimal ways. There are many ways to collect ideas; writing notebooks are only one. For example, Maggie Stiefvater, a young adult novelist, collects ideas for her novels by writing them in marker on her hand (and arms if she needs more space). Remember, the writing process is not about specific tools, but rather about working through the different phases.

Collecting is a playful part of the writing process. It allows us to follow our passions and indulge our curiosity about a topic. For me, it's one of the more essential parts of the process—I collect daily in my notebooks (see Figure 15.6).

Move to Make No. 5: Build curiosity.

Humans are wired to be curious. When we tap curiosity in students, we spark a primitive impulse. Collecting ought to be fun. It should make us excited and infuse a writing project with energy. If energy for writing is low in your class, consider the following ways to make collecting more meaningful to your students.

TAKING THE FIRST STEPS

- *Scan the QR code to peek inside my writing notebooks by watching the video minilesson I created. Consider the variety of ways writers collect ideas and how you can expand on these in your classroom.*

- *Start (or dust off) your own writing notebook and make a few entries.*

- *Explore some non-traditional ways to collect. Pay attention to students who do not have an affinity for their notebooks and explore different ways for them to collect ideas.*

PLANNING

Writers plan. For me, this is a different step in the writing process from collecting. I still use my notebook to capture a plan, but the process is more structured than when I collect. Planning involves thinking through the parts of a writing project. In addition to planning the parts, I also plan for research as well as the time line I foresee for completing the project.

In the planning phase, my notebook transforms from a junk drawer to a practice field. I'm gearing up for a new writing project, and I'm using my notebook to train. I'll make a game plan, capture specific notes, and sometimes even try a few lines to see if I can settle into the tone I want for the project.

Just as there are many ways to collect, there are many ways to plan for a writing project. Lots of students tell me they are "make-a-plan-in-my-head" kinds of writers. I usually respond by saying, "I need to let you in on a little secret. The older you get, the more you forget. So, this year you are going to become the kind of writer who jots down a plan. Trust me, you'll thank me when you start to forget things."

I usually get an eye-roll and a small snicker. I smile back and say, "Plus, as your teacher, I need to know what you're thinking so I can help you become a stronger writer. If your plan is only in your head, then I'll have a hard time helping you as a writer unless I become a mind reader."

In a lighthearted way, I let students know that making plans in their heads alone is not an option. This knowledge is essential for kids who need a little luring to write.

Move to Make No. 6: Make a plan.

There are lots of ways writers plan, and I allow students to choose what they prefer. Since many students have very little schema for how writers make plans, I begin by describing a couple of options and then give lots of examples. I encourage students to try one of the options discussed here.

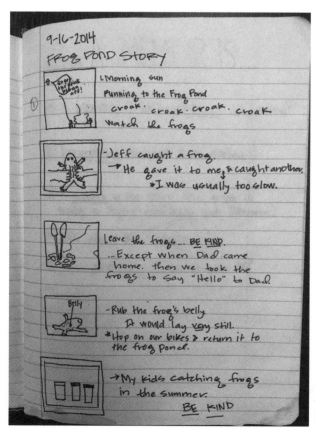

FIGURE 15.7
A storyboard from my notebook: a plan for a memoir

FIGURE 15.8
I used a storyboard to plan a fable.

Storyboards

Penny Kittle is an advocate of storyboards, and she has made me an advocate, too. Storyboards allow students to consider the main scenes or parts of a writing project. I like comparing them to the scene-selection options on DVDs, or to the scene-commercial-scene structure of TV shows. It is important to create your own storyboard so students can see how to use the tool for planning (see Figures 15.7 and 15.8).

Oral Storytelling

Many students can use a hand to plan a story—literally! By using our fingers to tell each part, we can develop a plan for our next writing project. We can teach students to use their hands to tell a story by raising the pointer finger and saying, "One time . . . " Then using the following fingers to say, "And then . . . ," "Suddenly . . . ," and "Finally . . . ." (See Figure 15.9.)

Another option is for students to jot a note down on the top of each page (or, for younger writers, to make a sketch on each page) to guide their writing. Feel free to add some draft paper to your writing center to scaffold students as they make writing plans. Scan the QR code for more information.

FIGURE 15.9
Anchor chart to hold "hands" for oral storytelling

TAKING THE FIRST STEPS

- *Use your hand to think through the parts of a story you might write. Use the following QR code to watch the video minilesson* Need a Hand to Tell a Story, *which can help guide you in thinking through your story. Consider how you can use this lesson with your students.*

- *Make a storyboard for a story you might write. Scan the following QR code to watch the video minilesson* Planning a Narrative *for guidance in creating your own storyboard. Consider how to use this lesson with your students.*

- *Add some draft paper to your writing center that will scaffold students as they plan their writing.*

DRAFTING

Unlike collecting and planning, the purpose of drafting is to create something to share with readers. Collecting and planning are the work that writers do to position themselves to write drafts for an audience. I believe this is essential for students to understand, especially those who need a little charming in order to write. They must understand that writers do some things to prepare them to write and other things to produce writing for an audience. To help students know what goes in and out of a notebook, I encourage them to follow this general rule:

> *If the writing is for you as a writer, it goes in your notebook. If you are creating something for others to read, then it goes outside of your notebook.*

Plans go inside of notebooks. Drafts go outside of notebooks. Writers do their best on first drafts. This is not a sloppy copy. Writers don't write poorly on purpose. They don't avoid using ending punctuation, nor do they ignore spelling rules.

It is true that strong writers draft fluently, not stopping to nitpick as they are writing first drafts. For example, as I draft this, I'm not sure if *nitpick* should be hyphenated (*nit-pick*) or written out as two words (*nit pick*). Rather than breaking my train of thought and turning to Google to find the answer, I'm going to keep drafting. It's not that I want my draft to be sloppy, but instead I don't want to break my train of thought. I'll make a note (in my writing notebook, which is sitting right next to me) and check it later. (For the record, it's *nitpick*.)

As a writer, I don't make sloppy copies. Right now, I'm writing this chapter for the first time. I'm doing my absolute best. I'm drafting with sentences and paragraphs. I'm following capitalization rules, and I'm crafting in a way to control the voice so that you won't stop reading! We must teach students to write *a best first draft*. In a best first draft, writers intentionally mold their words, doing their best work to develop meaning through craft and conventions.

There is a tension between writing your best and not being distracted by getting every little thing just right. It's a tightrope I walk as a writer: wanting to write my best, yet knowing drafting is discovery and exploration. There is a difference between writing well and aiming for perfection. I can write my best first draft *and* it can be messy. The point is, I do the best writing I can each time I write.

As an experienced writer, I've learned to recognize when I'm stifling myself. In these moments, I return to my notebook—my personal junk drawer. I write a few paragraphs or attempt to get a few fresh thoughts down on the page without the pressure of writing a best first draft.

Like the other steps in the writing process, drafting can be approached in as many ways as there are writers. Some, like me, are very intentional about craft and conventions in their first drafts. Others write quickly, creating a flash draft first and then sorting out the words and parts and then planning for a more intentional subsequent draft. Some writers draft on the computer, others use a legal pad and gel pen. Sometimes I draft by voice-recording a few lines as I drive to work. It is crucial to give students many different visions for the ways they can write best first drafts.

Move to Make No. 7: Write a draft in a way that works for you.

The following table outlines different ways to write a draft.

Google Drive Document	*Type a document in Google Drive. This allows easy collaboration between writers.*
Paper—legal pads, spiral notebooks	*Some writers prefer to draft by hand, preferring the slower pace. Sometimes a notebook is more portable for students than a device, allowing them to work on their writing in a variety of places.*
Draft Paper	*We can help scaffold students' understandings of different genres by creating draft paper that will help them follow genre conventions as they write. For example, if students are writing poetry, they can have paper with short lines to encourage line breaks.*
Google Slides	*Google Slides is a great way to organize nonfiction into different subtopics. I've been using Slides more often to help organize and script videos.*
Voice Recording	*When I don't have access to a way to write my thoughts, I'll record my voice. This isn't something that students will use very often, but it is a way to broaden our thinking about ways to write a draft.*
Scripts and Sketches	*As the definition of a writing project expands to encompass video and infographics, it is important for students to begin learning how to draft scripts that go beyond dialogue to include sound effects, image, and music.*

TAKING THE FIRST STEPS

- *Scan the following QR code to watch the video minilesson* Write Your Best First Draft, *which will help guide you in talking about best first drafts with students.*

- *Explore using different tools to write your own drafts. As you write, pay attention to how you balance the drafting tightrope of doing your best without stifling yourself as a writer.*

- *Add some draft paper to your writing center that will scaffold students in different genres. (See Figure 15.10.)*

Name	Page
	Date

Part

FIGURE 15.10
Sample draft paper

I'M DONE!

I mentioned previously that I struggled in my early days of writing workshop because I had a difficult time figuring out how to allow students to set their own writing pace. It seemed we all planned together and drafted together and revised together. (Except for those who did things more quickly than others—those students were often reading or chatting or doing homework for other classes while they waited for the next step.) Unintentionally, I became a gatekeeper for writers. They weren't allowed to go on until I explained what to do.

This isn't the best way for students to become stronger writers. They need practice, and lots of it. The writing process chart is arranged in a circular way to help students feel comfortable moving on to another writing project. Traditional charts are linear, but I know this isn't how I work as a writer. Sometimes I jump right into a draft. I've met plenty of students who jump into drafts without much forethought, too. I don't believe writers must begin with collecting followed by planning followed by drafting.

Most students already have a writing process in place. The key is to help them become stronger writers by refining the current process they are using. Arranging the parts of the process in a circle allows students to follow whatever course suits them best. No one phase of the writing process supersedes another. They are all important—we use all three phases as writers, and we can enter writing projects via any of them.

Putting Process into Action

Let's say we are studying a unit on short fiction. A student finishes a draft and says, "I'm done!"

I used to cringe when I heard those two little words. Often I responded by saying, "Writers are never done." Another favorite was, "You're not done, because when writers think they're done, they've only just begun!"

Although true, this advice was neither helpful nor encouraging. Once I started writing alongside students, I realized that "I'm done!" is actually a spot-on response to finishing a draft. It is not a slight thing to finish a draft. It deserves celebration. In my mind, party horns and cupcakes are involved. Frankly, I wouldn't feel very celebratory to anyone who reminded me, "Writers are never done."

Today, the conversation is a little different when a student says, "I'm done!" I typically high-five the student and say, "You finished your draft? Good job!" followed by a fist-bump and, "Doesn't it feel good to finish a draft? You should share it with someone."

You can imagine the smiles and the energy my responses incite. I continue to build excitement for the writing, then I point to the writing-process chart.

"Since you've finished this draft, you should get ready to write another," I say. "Selection Day isn't until the end of next week. I bet you'll be able to write two or three different stories before then."

The students begin the work again, starting with collecting or planning or drafting an entirely new project. This gives them the chance for more practice and allows them to work through the writing process at their own pace. By expecting students to write at least two different best first drafts for a unit of study, we can provide them with ample opportunity to practice.

Move to Make No. 8: Celebrate a finished draft and prepare to write another.

Be on the lookout for students who will simply make a few edits to their first draft. This isn't the point. The point is to have two *different* drafts on two *different* topics and to practice working as a writer. When I used to share a linear writing process with students, they'd typically write one draft, edit it, and say, "I'm done!" It was difficult to get them to keep writing because they felt they had accomplished the task.

TAKING THE FIRST STEPS

- *Create name tags for your students to place on the writing-process chart as they decide the work they will do as writers each day. This will allow you to visually monitor whether they are moving through the writing process with ease.*

- *Create an anchor chart with things writers can do when they think they are done (see Figure 15.11). This encourages students to celebrate in the middle of the writing process and energizes them to write another draft.*

SELECTION

After students have written more than one best first draft, it is time to move on to the Selection phase. Writers don't publish everything they write. I have written many articles that will stay in a drafts folder on my computer. They aren't worth my time to revise, edit, and publish (and they definitely aren't worth your time to read). They are, and always will be, drafts. *I'm done* with them, so to speak.

This can be a hard truth for some students to accept. They don't want to write drafts that might not "count." They want all their work to be published and fancy. Many kids from hard places see it as a waste of time and effort to write drafts that aren't "for anything."

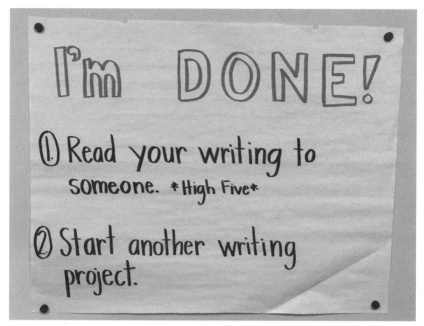

FIGURE 15.11
I'm Done! chart of things students can do after finishing a best first draft

Truthfully, this is a hard mindset to combat. In order to write well, we must practice. Practice for writers is drafting. We write draft after draft after draft and then we select one to take through the publishing process.

It is important to teach students how to select a draft worthy of sharing with an audience (see Figure 15.12). Once we get on the path to publication, the work can be brutal. On Selection Day, encourage students to follow these steps to find the draft they want to take to publication:

1. *Find a place to work and spread out.*

2. *Gather all your drafts.*

3. *Pile the drafts or put them around you.*

4. *Settle in and read your drafts, just like you do a book.*

5. *Take your time.*

6. *Make a thoughtful choice about the draft you want to share with a larger audience.*

7. *Move on to revision!*

Most writers have deadlines. Before creating a Selection Day, the only deadline my students had was the publication date for their final product. If students missed this deadline, it was too late to catch up. Today, students know that they must have two or more complete drafts by the Selection Day. If they don't, we're able to make a plan (recess, lunch, a call home) to get the writing work done. There's no damage done, because we realize early the need for better time management.

Move to Make No. 9: Establish a Selection Day.

At the end of writing workshop on Selection Day, plan to have a Selection Celebration. Mary Lee Hahn introduced me to this idea. She asks her students to bring the draft they've decided to see toward publication to the share session. The class sits in a circle and students each share the title of their drafts and why they decided to put the effort into the work. Everyone applauds, and students follow the energy into revision, editing, and publication.

FIGURE 15.12
Third-grade students reading their drafts and preparing to select one to take to publication

TAKING THE FIRST STEPS

- *Help your students develop a vision for the selection process by sharing the video minilesson* Selecting a Draft for Publication.

- *Allow students time to make their selections and then to share the reasons for selecting them. Giving these reasons always energizes students to write.*

REVISING

Writers revise and edit. They are two different stages of the writing process, with two distinct purposes. Revision is the part of the writing process when writers focus on clarifying meaning. When preparing a draft for publication, this is very important. Revision helps writers to strengthen their meanings by making sure their language is clear and they are following formatting conventions.

Revision isn't easy for the beginning writer. Nor is it easy for teachers to let the discovery process happen. It's why we search Pinterest for revision checklists and one more idea for how to help students revise.

Donald Murray's classic advice for helping students to discover meaning during revision is to model the process for them. He suggests allowing students to see the process unfold in real time. Teachers can write on chart paper, smart boards, or under document cameras. It doesn't really matter where we write, just so students are able to see the revision process unfold. When students see teachers wrestle with their own writing and tease a mess into meaning, they learn how to engage in significant revision.

I've met my share of students who do not like to revise. When I share my writing and my revision process with them, it is like adding ointment to a wound. Watching a teacher work as a writer has the power to soothe and soften attitudes toward revision. It is more powerful than listening to someone talk about the process and much more effective than filling out a revision worksheet. When students see teachers revise, they begin to accept it as a natural and necessary part of the typical writing process rather than a penalty reserved for flawed writers.

Move to Make No. 10: Model revision with your own writing in front of students.

Revision Tools

When students have access to revision tools, they are one step closer to revising. Although these tools represent a powerful step toward revision, just having access to them is not enough for students to engage in the process meaningfully. Students must first learn that revision is not a process of correcting, but a process of discovery. Murray writes, "When revision is encouraged, not as a punishment but as a natural process in the exploration of the text to discover meaning, then many basic writers become motivated to revise" (1981, 89).

Revision is about finding meaning. In our hurry-up world, it is easy for students to believe they know the meaning before they start writing. But writing doesn't work this way; writing is a *means* to discovering important ideas. Before students turn to revision tools, they must discover the core meaning of their writing. This is done by rereading what they've written and looking for the words, phrases, and sentences that matter most.

Ralph Fletcher has a great chapter in his book *How Writers Work* (2000), written just for young writers, about rereading. It's an easy action to overlook, but as a writer, I do more rereading than I do stringing words together. Rereading is necessary for writers to discover meaning. Once students have discovered their meaning, they can begin using revision tools to clarify it. The following chart outlines some of the tools I share with students in order to boost revision.

TOOL	HOW IT ENCOURAGES REVISION
Carat	The carat encourages writers to add a few words to their drafts. With younger students, this often leads to one-word revisions, where students add missing words, replace incorrect ones, or insert adjectives to give readers a stronger picture (e.g., adding blonde to hair, changing went to dashed).
Spider Legs	Spider legs are among my favorite revision tools for encouraging students to add an entire sentence or two to their writing. I first learned about this strategy from the All-Write!!! Consortium.
	You will need to cut strips of paper about one-and-a-half inches wide and eleven inches long. These are the "spider legs," and you'll want to have tons. I prefer to put them in a small basket with a roll of tape. Then I put the basket in the writing center or another place that is accessible to students.
	To use spider legs, students decide where they can add a sentence or two to their drafts. Then they write the revision on the spider leg and tape it to the draft. The long strips hang off the edges of the draft, looking like spider legs.
	Since the strips are thin and attached with a single piece of tape, they do not cover the other words on the draft. Students love to see the "legs" dangling from their drafts, so they often add more than one.
Coding	When students want to add more to their drafts but they don't have room, they can use a code. For example, they might add an asterisk where they want to add dialogue to the draft. Then, on another sheet of paper (or in their notebooks), they draw a corresponding asterisk and write the lines of dialogue. If they want to revise another part of the draft, then they use another symbol. Numbers also work well as a coding system.
	This strategy encourages lengthy revisions and helps students to add text even if there isn't room on the original draft.
Sticky Notes	I'm not sure what it is about sticky notes, but it seems that when nothing else encourages revision, a sticky note will. I like to have some oversized sticky notes (especially ones with preprinted lines) when I need some magical enticement for revision. I ask students to find a part of their draft they can add more to and then give them a sticky note. If they are writing a narrative, I might say, "See if you can fill this sticky note with the inside story." The idea of filling the sticky note resonates with many students and they typically rise to the challenge.

TOOL	HOW IT ENCOURAGES REVISION
Colored Pens	*Students often have access to colored pens but rarely get to use them. Using that neon-orange gel pen that they just love can be a strong incentive for revising their drafts. This strategy makes students' revisions pop out from their drafts.*
Track Changes	*On Google Drive and MS Word, students can automatically track all their changes and leave comments in the document. This allows them to see exactly where and how much revision they have done.*

Move to Make No. II: Provide students with tools to encourage revision.

Significant Revision

Significant revision hinges on writers making a choice about how to revise. This is different than deciding which revision tool to use. Writers typically do four things to clarify meaning: delete, add, move, or replace. The following table includes some ways writers use these four options to revise but you can come up with some of your own ideas as well.

Move to Make No. 12: Make revision simple and satisfying.

Add	*Add missing scenes or information.* *Add specific kinds of details. For example, in narrative writing students can add action, dialogue, or thinking. They can also add setting details. In non-narrative writing, students can add quotes, statistics, facts, or commentary. In poetry, students can add sensory details or figurative language. It is important to teach students to add specific kinds of details.*
Delete	*Delete unnecessary scenes, inaccurate or untrue details, and parts that do not add to the meaning.*
Move	*Reorder scenes for clarity or emphasis and combine sentences.*
Replace	*Replace an unsatisfying beginning or ending, a boring scene, or a subtopic that doesn't connect to the meaning.*

1. *Writers discover the big meaning of their drafts by rereading and thinking.*

2. *Writers select revision tools to help clarify the meaning.*

3. *Writers choose the best revision options for their drafts.*

It is possible to entice students to write through revision opportunities. The key is to wrap strong arms around the revision process so students get the chance to revise in significant and meaningful ways.

> **Favorite Books to Help Understand the Revision Process**
>
> *Real Revision* by Kate Messner
>
> *How Writers Work* by Ralph Fletcher
>
> *The Revision Toolbox* by Georgia Heard
>
> *After the End* by Barry Lane

TAKING THE FIRST STEPS

- *Create a place for revision tools in your classroom. Allow students access to the tools without being a gatekeeper.*

- *Scan the following QR code to check out the video minilesson 4 Revision Choices and learn ways to talk about the four revision decisions with students.*

EDITING

This step of the writing process is focused on making writing align with Standard English as much as possible. At the same time, the priority of writing workshop is teaching students to write well, not simply to hew to conventions.

When I was brand new to writing workshop, I was at a study group where a second-grade teacher shared about posting her students' writing on the hallway bulletin board. This teacher was nearing the end of her career and she said it was the first time she had ever posted less-then-perfect student writing. "Always before I made students correct every single grammatical error," she said. The group applauded her for honoring children's development by posting their writing without demanding perfection.

"Don't clap yet," she laughed. "You have to hear the rest of the story."

When she returned to school the next morning, someone had taken a red marker and made thick proofreader's marks on every single piece of student writing. The teacher stood in front of the corrected stories feeling embarrassed and mad. As she pulled down each story, she started to cry. She felt reprimanded by the red marks. Then she thought of her students. Even though the conventions weren't perfect, her students had grown so much as writers. They were excited about adding dialogue and action to their stories. They loved stretching "hundred-dollar" words and celebrated being independent writers.

She paused and looked at a story in her hand. Five words were corrected, but every word-wall word was spelled conventionally. Her students stretched words and took the time to find the conventional spelling of grade-level words. They were proud of their stories and excited to see them "go public" in the main hall.

In a few minutes school would start, and the second graders were going to find that their stories didn't measure up to someone's standards. She rushed to finish taking down the remaining red-marked stories. As she dried her eyes and repaired her mascara, she thought, "We're just going to publish again."

Later in class, she told her students that they were going to make their stories look fancier. She found legal-sized colored paper and printed fancy borders around it. She gave students access to colored felt-tipped pens. She even broke out the glitter (and smiled sinisterly to herself: now the night custodian would be too busy to work a thick red marker on student work). Before returning the now-fancy student work to the bulletin board, she typed a letter to add as well that focused on everything the students knew as writers, framing each reader's view.

"I decided there was no reason for me to be embarrassed," said the teacher to the study group. "Their writing looked like second-grade writing. They are the most confident writers I have ever taught. Their conventions might not be perfect, but their writing is so much stronger than anything my former students have ever written. I decided to defend them as writers, as well as my instructional decisions."

I wish I knew this teacher's name so I could thank her. Her story changed me. I decided to stop insisting on perfection when students went public with their writing. I realized that when student writing goes public, we must be ready to defend it in the world. It's not perfection that matters. It's growth and strength that matters most.

Move to Make No. 13: Stand up for imperfect student use of conventions.

There will always be people in this world who wield thick red pens and look to correct mistakes. It takes a strong teacher to be able to shift the perspective from what students *aren't* doing to what they *are* doing as writers. Although I don't have the original letter the teacher in the previous story added to her bulletin board, I have several that have been inspired by her. Below is a bare-bones, fill-in-the-blank version of a letter to post alongside your next writing projects that are going public but are not yet perfect.

Hello Readers!

We are so happy you paused to read our writing. We've been working hard as writers and learning a lot about how writers craft _____ (genre). Check out the way we work words by:

(List teaching points: e.g., learning to write specific actions to help readers make a movie in their minds. How many specific actions can you find in our stories?)

We've also been learning about conventions. See if you can spot these in our work: (List teaching points: e.g., interrogative, exclamatory, declarative, and imperative sentences.)

Finally, we know there's no such thing as a perfect writer. All writers must keep practicing in order to grow and make their writing more meaningful. This is the best writing we could do and still meet the deadline. We won't be making the same errors in a month. (We'll be making new errors!) This is okay, because writers grow best when they take risks and learn from their mistakes.

Happy reading,
_____ *(room number)*

If the writer is five, then the writing should reflect it. This step in the writing process is about getting as close to conventional as appropriate for students.

Peer Editing

I joke that I was a decent speller until I started reading so much student writing. Now I know better: I ask Sam, the top speller in our house, whenever I'm unsure how to spell something.

I can easily overlook misspellings, so I like to have others read my notes and other handwritten items before I send them out in the world. If I'm working on a computer, I trust spell-check, but still use proofreaders for things like my newsletters and articles.

This is true for all writers. We have proofreaders and more formal copyeditors. I think it's a misconception to lead students to believe that they must catch all editing needs on their own. Another set of eyes will always increase the quality of proofreading.

Move to Make No. 14: Teach students to be effective peer editors.

Students have a tendency to simply swap papers when in the editing phase. I've learned a more effective approach. Students sit shoulder to shoulder with the writing between them. The writer has the pen, and the peer editor is ready to pay attention to details. The writer begins by slowly reading and the peer editor follows along. When they spot an error, they point it out and discuss it, then the writer corrects it. If the writer decides the point in question doesn't need to be fixed, then he or she leaves it as it is; the writer always has the final say. This strategy allows students to spot a significant amount of errors by forcing two sets of eyes to slow down and pay attention to conventions. (See Figure 15.13.)

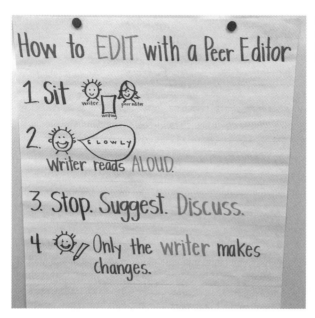

FIGURE 15.13
A chart to guide students through the peer-editing process

Often it is through peer editing that students are enticed into the editing process. They enjoy talking with one another and sometimes more readily take advice from one another than the teacher. Of course, there are always a few students who do not work well with peers. This doesn't change the fact that it is valuable to get another set of eyes for editing. Some students are enticed by selecting an adult in the school to peer edit. I've never met another adult in school who refuses to be a "peer" editor. In fact, I've known custodians, bus drivers, and office assistants who have enjoyed the task.

TAKING THE FIRST STEPS

- *Scan the following QR code to watch* How to Peer Edit *and use the video minilesson to give students a strong vision for the way peer editing ought to go.*

- *Check out Jeff Anderson's classic grammar books,* Everyday Editing *and* Mechanically Inclined, *for more ideas about weaving grammar instruction into writing workshop.*

GOING PUBLIC

Finally, writers share their writing with an audience. Make certain to offer students audiences both inside and outside the classroom walls. It is also important to provide them with the opportunity to go global with their words. Allowing students to share via social networking sites helps them realize that words matter all over the world.

In the book I cowrote with Christi Overman, *Celebrating Writers* (2012), we shared forty ideas for formally celebrating the writing process with students. Formal celebrations do not need to happen often; one, two, or three times a year is sufficient. They fuel writers in ways other kinds of celebrations do not.

Following is a list of my personal top ten formal celebrations.

Move to Make No. 15: Host a formal writing celebration.

TOP TEN FORMAL CELEBRATIONS

1. Toast

In Independent Writing, *Colleen Cruz (2004) suggests gathering students with small glasses of juice and offering them a toast. You can toast to students' learning, to their success in completing their writing projects, and to the community of writers at large. "Hear! Hear!" the writers say, and then the floor is open to anyone who wants to share about the impact of writing workshop.*

2. Silent Celebration

Students place their writing alongside a response sheet throughout the classroom. Moving from one seat to another, students read and respond to each work in silence. At the end, students rejoice by reading their comments and then sharing one or two of their favorites with the whole class.

3. Poetry Jam

Students each bring a poem to the celebration. They sit in a circle and have one person begin by reading his or her poem. The next person to read is determined by linking his or her poem to the previous poem. For example, if the first reader shares a poem about playing ball with her dog, then the next reader might be someone who also wrote about a dog or perhaps about baseball. Be creative, and remember that poets often snap rather than clap to show their appreciation for a poem.

4. Writers Helping Writers

In this celebration, students determine something about which they would like to receive feedback regarding their current writing project. For example, a student may bring two different leads to the celebration to figure out which one is most effective. Perhaps a student is concerned about whether there are enough facts in the informative article he or she is writing, or whether his or her opinions are clear in a persuasive letter.

5. Bulletin Board
Students complete a written reflection and then display their writing next to it. By using page protectors or plastic frames, students can easily change the writing they display throughout the year. Also consider including a letter from you, the teacher, to the reader directing attention to the learning students are experiencing (see sample letter on page 106).

6. Author's Chair
This is a good choice if you're short on time to plan something more elaborate. Students take turns sitting in the Author's Chair and read aloud a portion of their writing, then others offer oral or written responses. For the chair itself, you can paint a flea-market find or be creative: milk crates, paint buckets, and old rocking chairs can all hold writers up in celebration.

7. Campfire
Stories love to dance around a campfire. Set up a campfire, either real or pretend, and give students a chance to share their stories. Of course, s'mores are a perfect way to rejoice during this kind of celebration. Students may share—or complete—reflections in addition to sharing their stories.

8. Family Writing Workshop
Invite families to attend an after-school writing workshop. Plan a minilesson and give families a chance to write together. Feel free to confer and talk with families as they write. End the workshop with a share session, first giving families a chance to share together and then inviting writers to share with the whole group. When scheduled near the beginning of the year, this celebration provides an opportunity to help parents understand and experience writing workshop.

9. Author Interviews
Students plan to interview their writing partners for this celebration, which helps students to understand the writing process in a more personal way. Plan to share a few interviews each day across a week or two. To go all out, stage a talk-show atmosphere with unique chairs and microphones. Another option is to videotape the interviews and share them via YouTube.

10. Small Group
Students share their writing projects and offer responses and reflections in a small group of three to five writers.

The positive feedback that comes with going public is often what makes the hard work of the writing process worthwhile for students.

TAKING THE FIRST STEPS

- *Look ahead on your calendar and make a plan for a formal writing celebration. Add it to your calendar today and share the date with guests.*

- *Take time to snap a few photos during the celebration and post them to social media. Include captions that highlight the key things students know about being writers.*

CHAPTER 16: WRITING PROJECTS THAT MAKE YOU WANT TO WRITE

Writers work best when they have writing projects rather than pieces. I never understood what *pieces* meant, anyway. Pieces of writing makes me think of pieces of a puzzle. Writing is complicated enough, why jumble it by making only pieces? Pieces of writing make pieces of a writer.

Our classrooms need wholehearted writers, not pieces of writers. Writers work on writing *projects*—this is real work, and as such it can seem daunting. In an effort to make writing more manageable, sometimes we turn to short writing assignments. If these assignments don't connect to a meaningful purpose, some kids will write less. Rather than attempting to make writing assignments, let's engage kids in making big, important stuff that they can't wait to work on and share.

It may seem counterintuitive to encourage students to work on writing projects when they are hesitant to write, but I've come to believe that the best thing we can do to entice kids to write more is to empower them to be excited about their writing projects. To be energized for a writing project, writers must have choice.

This means there won't be identical writing projects in the classrooms (something that used to stress me out—I couldn't imagine having ninety different writing projects happening in my seventh-grade language arts classes.)

Choice is a double-edged sword. It can be both a benefit and a liability. It is a benefit because it is the best way to engage students in writing. When students are invested in writing projects, they are willing to write. I found ways to manage choice in order to tap the benefits.

However, I also noticed that there were a few kids who seemed stumped by choice. You've seen these kids, too: they can never find a topic to write about, or they don't know who would want to read their writing. For kids coming from hard places, lack of choice is often something to fight against, while too much choice can be overwhelming. This was the root of the problem between Jordan and his math teacher— just picking from a list of assignments was too much choice for him. In both cases, no choice or too much choice, we are likely to evoke a fear-based response from students. During writing workshop, this looks like a kid with little or no stamina.

Move to Make No. 16: Offer choice in writing projects.

Choice is an essential move to enticing students to write. However, for the kids coming from hard places, we need to take care when extending choice. To find how to offer choice without it being overwhelming, let's consider the decisions writers make for any writing project. (See anchor chart in Figure 16.1.)

1. *Who will read my writing? (Audience)*

2. *What will I write about? (Topic)*

3. *What will I make? (Genre)*

4. *Why am I writing? (Purpose)*

An *assignment* is given when the teacher makes all four of these decisions and the writer makes none. A *piece* is written when only some of these decisions are made, because only pieces of a writing project were decided.

We entice writers when they have some of the decision-making power. They don't have to make all the decisions, but they ought to make some. For example, if everyone is going to write to persuade, then the purpose for writing has been limited, but maybe students can decide what genre they will write in. Perhaps they are asked to write about a school issue. In this case, since the topic is limited, maybe keep the audience open.

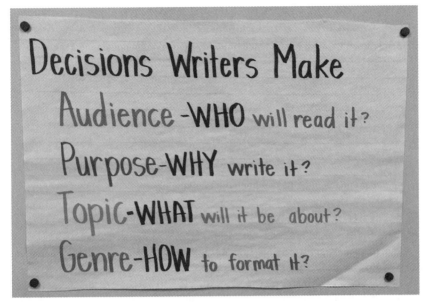

FIGURE 16.1
Decisions writers make for a writing project

DIGGING DEEPER INTO DECISIONS

Audience: Who Will Read My Writing?

When working on a writing project, writers have an audience in mind. Many kids from hard places make the false assumption that no one cares about their stories. They believe no one wants to read their writing.

I'm reminded of when Jay first joined our family. He was always surprised to find us watching him. At dinner one time, I put the hot sauce in front of his plate when I sat the table. "How you know I like tha'?" he asked.

"You use it every night! I thought it should always be on the table at dinner so you can use it when you want it."

"You's always watchin' me," Jay said, shaking his head in disbelief.

When kids grow up nourished, they make eye contact with their parents all the time. Sam, our son who has been with us from birth, used to make sure I was watching before eating his dinner. It's been more than three years that Jay has been part of our family, and he is just now starting to make regular eye contact with us. Andy coaches Jay's football team, and this is the first year that Jay will look to Andy before a play to see if he's watching. Yet Jay's still surprised by our attention.

I missed a football game once because I was taking Hannah shopping for her birthday. Andy texted me the highlights of Jay's game. When we came home, I said, "There's the guy who ran for the winning touchdown!"

"How'd you know?" Jordan asked.

I smiled and looked at Andy.

"Dad tol' you that?"

Andy laughed. "Of course I told her that! It was awesome."

Jordan beamed.

If it still takes Jordan by surprise that his stories mean something to his parents, think how much harder it is for our students who are still in hard places to believe their writing matters to an audience.

Move to Make No. 17: Convince students there is an audience that cares about reading their writing.

Part of enticing writers is helping them to know and consider their audiences. An audience affects many of the decisions a writer makes. One way to help students consider different audiences is to create a chart as a class identifying different kinds (see Figure 16.2). Don't hesitate to list specific names in each of the categories; kids need to know real people care about their writing.

FIGURE 16.2
Use these categories to help students name specific people (or groups of people) as potential audiences.

CLASSROOM	LOCAL	GLOBAL
Classmates	Other classrooms	Blog readers
Teacher	Family members	Twitter followers
Paraprofessionals	Principal	Connected classrooms
Volunteers	School personnel	

BE REAL

Many kids who are hesitant to write are a lot like Jordan: They don't know that someone cares about their stories. They can listen to the lesson about audience and even participate in offering names to add to the chart, but they can't imagine anyone wants to hear what they have to say. The best thing we can do for kids who come from hard places is to give them the experience of someone caring about the words they write.

In the end, students need an opportunity to share their words with their audiences. It is easy for this reality to fall through the cracks. Don't let it. We get busy, and then the next unit of study rolls around and the writing never lands in the hands of the intended audience. Make a commitment now to let students share their writing with audiences. It is the only way they will learn their voices have impact and be willing to fill a blank page again and again.

Topic: What Will I Write About?

Writers have their preferred topics. Patricia MacLachlan, for example, writes about the prairie. In fact, when I heard her speak, she pulled a baggie of dirt out of her pocket to show the audience. She literally carried the prairie with her. Rick Riordan writes about mythology. I write about teaching writers.

When it comes to topics, it's important for students to realize that they don't always have to come up with new ones. When Sam was in fourth grade, he wrote a narrative about crashing his skateboard and breaking his collarbone. He wrote an informative article about skateboarding gear. He wrote a persuasive letter to Andy and me about why he needed skater shoes. He wrote skateboarding poems, skateboarding fiction, and skateboarding notebook entries.

At the same time, Sam explored a variety of topics in addition to skateboarding—the effects of pollution from different kinds of transportation; speed trains; how to pick up a split in bowling; the newest airplane designs. He also worked intermittently on his graphic novel, *Toilet Man*, and enjoyed leaving notes in his sibling's lockers.

Kids with little stamina often get stuck on choosing a topic to write about. We've all heard the infamous lament: "But I have nothing to write about!" Don't mistake this as an invitation to give students a topic. You already know they aren't going to like anything you suggest. It's easier for students to have nothing to write about, because then they have an excuse not to write.

Do not give up. Instead, help students learn how to select topics. By asking students to be on the lookout for topics, we can encourage them to select ones that are meaningful and timely.

I often write about ways to engage students in the process of topic selection. We can make collages on chart paper with primary students or collect lists of topic ideas in notebooks with older students. Before we know it, we can have charts and notebooks filled with ideas of things to write about. However, just like Jay and his math assignments, the long list of possibilities has the potential to be too much.

I think about Rheece, the student who failed my seventh-grade language arts class in the first nine weeks of my teaching career. He was kicked off of the football team. As I started to repair our relationship and get to know Rheece, I didn't ask him to make lists or maps or sketches in his notebook. I just talked with him, and I listened to his responses.

He didn't have much to say to me. Not only was his reality dark, but I wasn't on his list of people he wanted to spend time talking with. It felt like a case of too little, too late. Still, I kept talking and listening.

As a coach, I often work with students I've never met before. Some of my favorite work is to model writing workshop for teachers. Within the workshop time, my favorite thing to do is to confer with students about their writing. Without fail, the students I gravitate to are usually those who need the most enticing.

These are the students I'm thinking about as I write this section. They don't need more lists of ideas. They don't need another kind of notebook page to create. They don't need someone to give them another topic idea. They just need to believe in the ideas they already have.

Move to Make No. 18: Validate student topic ideas.

Rheece needs to know he can write about playing football in the backyard with his brother and dad. Rosalee needs to know she can write about saying goodbye to her dad when he was deployed with the Air Force. Zane needs to know he can write about the haunted house he helped his neighbor decorate. Josh needs to know he can write about fishing off his grandpa's pier. Bella needs to know she can write about making cookies with her aunt.

Too often, students have people in their lives who tell them the things they do or like are stupid. It's not a surprise, then, that they think their topic ideas are stupid.

Rarely do I ask kids to make giant lists in their notebooks or look at collages with lots of writing ideas to find a writing topic. Instead, I have a conversation with them. I find out what they like to do, and I validate their interests. I smile when they talk about fishing. My eyes widen when they tell me they build with Legos or they play with train tracks or they love to dress up like a doctor or construction worker or the tooth fairy. I promise to keep my lips sealed when they tell me about their secret hideouts or the times they were naughty.

I listen well. I ask questions to get (or keep) the conversation going. I listen more. I react with laughter or surprise or sadness. Eventually, students keep talking without my prompting. It is then that I say, "It sounds like you've found something to write about."

They wrinkle their noses and shake their heads. They don't believe me. I slide a sheet of paper onto their desks, or we open a Google document. "Really," I say. "This is something worth writing. Will you try it?"

It's a fragile move. In fact, it seems almost silly to call it a move to entice writers. I sit next to a kid who doesn't have anything to write about. I ask a few questions, then wait. She starts talking and I keep her talking. I react. She smiles. Then I say, "Will you try writing this?"

I'm genuine with my validation. I'm patient with my listening. I refuse to rush. The student either writes or refuses. Usually words are put on the page, but even if they're verbalized I know I'm one step closer to enticing a student to write. I'm one step closer to knowing a little more about what matters. I'm one step closer to building a relationship that will allow the student to trust me with his or her stories.

Genre: What Will I Make?

In today's classrooms, genre is usually teacher-driven. Some curricula have been constricted to include one unit each on opinion, informative, and narrative writing. There is a difference between genre and categories of writing. Opinion writing is not a genre: Op-eds, persuasive letters, and persuasive essays are genres of opinion writing. Informative writing isn't a genre: "All about" books, feature articles, and public service announcements are genres of informative writing. Narrative writing isn't a genre: Small-moment stories, realistic fiction, and memoir are genres of narrative writing.

I believe that the most powerful writing is a combination of opinion, informative, and narrative. The lines of these categories are blurred, which is why genre knowledge is important to writers. The most powerful opinion writing usually includes a story, a narrative that makes the reader feel a connection and care as a human. My favorite narrative writing weaves in information. The book you are reading includes all three categories of writing and fits in the professional development genre.

Move to Make No. 19: Build genre knowledge.

Genre knowledge helps us write well. As students develop a stronger awareness of genre, they can make wiser choices as writers.

TAKE TIME FOR IMMERSION

When I got married, I wanted to sew my own wedding dress. To do this, I needed to figure out how my favorite dresses were made. In the dressing rooms of bridal shops, I'd turn gowns inside out and examine the seams. I took note of the number of layers under the skirt and the different types of beading on the bodice. I spent time with pattern books and scoured fabric stores. In short, I looked closely at the way wedding gowns were made.

Writers do something like this, too, but with mentor texts instead of wedding gowns. When students are writing in a specific genre, it is important for them to take some time to figure out how the genre works by immersing themselves in it. It's important for students to figure out how to make the kind of writing they want to make.

When Barb Bean taught fourth grade, she explained the concept of immersion to her students using milk and cookies as an example. "Whenever I eat cookies," she said, holding up a cookie, "I have to immerse them in milk." She then dunked the cookie in a glass of milk and popped it in her mouth.

"Yuuummmmm!" the class said in unison.

Writers dunk themselves in the genre they want to make. They ask themselves, What do I notice that makes this the kind of writing I want to try? As students make choices based on genre, they gain power as writers.

PROVIDE SPACE FOR GENRE CHOICE

Consider the writing projects students complete over the course of a year. How often do students have the time they really need to select the genre? Think about how to shift a unit of study to make this time. For example, rather than a personal narrative unit, perhaps you could shift to a broader narrative unit, letting students choose to write a personal narrative, memoir, or realistic fiction writing project. When I look at the units of study across a year, I try to ensure there are both genre-based and non-genre-based units for students.

Purpose: Why Am I Writing?

Purpose has the potential to come from the heart of the writer. The stronger our purpose, the more motivated we are to write. Sometimes the purpose is straightforward, like when we write to inform. Other times the purpose is closer to our bones, such as a public service announcement to encourage a food drive to battle childhood hunger. The more personal the purpose, the more likely the writer will approach the writing project with passion and commitment.

It's not enough to write because the teacher says to write. Let's help students find important and personal reasons to write. This book has been stirring for a long time, but it wasn't until I had a strong and unshakable purpose that I really buckled down and plowed through a draft. Once I knew why I was writing—because I believe that when kids write their stories they are able to live their dreams, touch lives, and make the world a better place, *and* because I believe that teachers are sometimes the last hope for kids to know their lives are worthy—I became able to write with a vengeance. I want to encourage teachers to keep helping kids live the best version of their stories as possible.

As my purpose attached itself to my heart, it became impossible for me not to write this book. The same is true for our students. We want to help them define clear and passionate purposes so it's impossible for them not to write.

Move to Make No. 20: Find personal reasons to write.

DEFINING A PURPOSE

One of the best ways to support students in defining a purpose for their writing projects is to ask them, "Why are you writing this?" Their answers give you instant insight into whether they have ownership to the project. A few other questions to get to the heart of purpose include the following:

- *Why is this writing project important?*
- *Why does this writing project matter to you?*
- *How will this writing project matter to others?*

You can ask these questions in writing workshop in several ways. They can become part of your conversations during conferences, and you can also use them as inspiration for share sessions. Students can talk with their writing partners or share with the whole group about the purpose behind their writing projects.

RICH WRITING PROJECTS

As long as we're carving out time for writing, let's make sure students are working on meaningful and engaging projects. As teachers, we must be strict with ourselves to allow space for students to make some of the choices in a writing project. When students become more attached to their projects, they develop greater self-confidence, and the impact this can have on their writing is impressive.

TAKING THE FIRST STEPS

- *Use these video minilessons to help students develop authentic writing projects:* What Will You Make in Writing Workshop? Writers Filter, *and* Write a Slice.

- *Create a space to collect feedback from audiences outside of the classroom walls. This can be a bulletin board, a corner of your newsletter, a highlight on your Facebook page, or a Twitter post with a special hashtag.*

- *Remember that listening is an act of teaching writing. Put aside the pressure for students to produce pages and pages of writing. Believe that your conversations and validation of topics is a worthwhile use of your time. This might be the most important work you do all day—giving kids permission to believe that their lives matter.*

CHAPTER 17:
STRETCH MENTORS
TO MEET NEEDS

've been looking at other professional books the way thieves case a joint for their next heist. I'm looking for structures I can swipe, a way to organize this section of the book that will make it accessible to you. I haven't filled out a graphic organizer, making sure each thought is mapped out. I haven't made an outline. I haven't even kept notes about different features to include. I've just been looking.

Sometimes I think we make mentors more complicated than they need to be. Writers naturally gravitate to mentors. The first year Andy took our boys to the Indy 500, he sent me a photo of Sam (see Figure 17.1).

When I saw the photo my first thought was, "Sam found a new mentor text!" Ticket scalpers are prolific on race day at the Indy 500. Regardless of how you feel about ticket scalping, it is obvious that their signs were mentor texts for Sam. Let's break it down:

1. *He used a piece of paper towel to make the sign. Recycled paper is a trademark of most scalpers.*

2. *He wrote a large title, modeled after the common sign, "We NEED Tickets."*

3. *He wrote a subtitle. (He wasn't going to risk losing his tickets!)*

4. *He shared the sign with his audience.*

Being impressed by Sam's use of a mentor text, it took me a moment to regain my wits as a parent. "Please tell me you didn't let him take money from people!"

Andy chuckled. "Of course not! The people parked around us thought he was hysterical and told him to go out by the road. I didn't let him, though. The last thing we need is Sam thinking he can make money by holding a sign." This is true. Sam has an entrepreneur's spirit. Ticket scalping and panhandling do not need to be on his list of creative business ventures.

Teaching students to use mentor texts doesn't have to be complicated. Feel free to use Sam's example with your students. Pull up an image of a ticket scalper and pair it with the image of Sam. Your students will see the similarities. Then

FIGURE 17.1
Sam was inspired by mentor texts at the Indy 500. The fine print reads, "We have tickets and we need money. THE TICKETS ARE NOT FOR SALE."

encourage them to use a mentor when they write. We can expect to see students being inspired by other mentors through the following:

- *Topic choices*
- *Titles*
- *First lines*
- *Illustrations*
- *Adding expert quotes*

Add some more ideas to this list. How can your students be inspired by mentor texts? Learning to use a mentor is about learning to model your writing after another writer.

Move to Make No. 21: Stretch mentors for a variety of inspiration.

FINDING A MENTOR

It's not enough to say, "Writers use mentors." We must help students claim writing mentors for themselves.

Move to Make No. 22: Support students in finding and claiming a writing mentor.

Mentors for Primary Writers

The youngest writers love to make books like their favorite authors. David Shannon, Kevin Henkes, Mo Willems, and Ashley Spires are some of my favorite mentors for primary students. Both their illustrations and texts offer exceptional mentoring opportunities.

It can be overwhelming to consider an entire book as a mentor. To help students learn to use mentors in a meaningful way, narrow the focus of the mentor text. For example, one way to entice students to write is to have them make a page like an author (see Figure 17.2). My son, Sam is a long-time reader of Jeff Kinney, Dav Pilkey, and Jim Davis. As a primary writer, his illustrations typically favored pen sketches and humor. As he has grown, most of his informal writing still includes sketches. It is Sam's way of adding humor.

If you pair Sam's page alongside a page from *Diary of a Wimpy Kid,* your students will be struck by many similarities. When students see this pairing of texts, using a mentor text becomes accessible.

Move to Make No. 23: Focus on a small part of the mentor text.

Mentors for Intermediate Writers

As students progress to mostly using words to craft their writing projects, the mentors we select should also reflect this move. Intermediate writing students are also writing in a wider variety of genres, so their needs for mentors are diverse. Because of this, Amy Ludwig VanDerwater put together a Padlet for teachers to share and find strong mentor texts in a variety of genres and interests. If you need to put your hands on a solid mentor text, you may want to begin here: https://padlet.com/AmyLV/WWMentorTexts.

If students are looking for a nonfiction mentor, I'm quick to connect them with magazines for kids. *National Geographic for Kids* and *Sports Illustrated for Kids* are two of my favorite titles. They both have excellent websites, too.

Seymour Simon and Gail Gibbons are solid mentors for young nonfiction writers. Both writers have numerous titles about diverse topics. Their craft is exquisite. Every time I introduce them to students, I end up learning more about how to craft nonfiction. It's fantastic! In addition, Seymour Simon has a strong web presence. He is active on Twitter and very generous to teachers.

Focusing on just a small part of the mentor texts remains a good idea at this stage. A tailored focus is charming for kids who are hesitant to write. It doesn't matter if we are looking at the covers of books, studying the facial expressions of characters in illustrations, or learning how to write thesis statements: When we place the spotlight on a single focus of a mentor text, we help students learn to use a mentor and apply the concepts to their own writing.

Mentors shouldn't be limited. Any author a student has a connection to can become a mentor. I love to encourage students who are "all done" writing to do a little research into their favorite writers. As they learn information about these writers' personal lives and writing processes, they begin to develop a connection.

It doesn't take much research to stumble across the truth that writers write more than they need. Writers write and write and write, and when they "finish" one project, they begin a new one. Providing a little time for students to learn about a favorite author is another way to encourage students to do the same. Researching favorite writers can also provide students with a productive buffer between writing projects. Students who are tentative to write may need a little space between drafts.

In writing as in other aspects of life, the company we keep influences the work we do. As writers, it is important to make sure we surround ourselves with high-quality companions.

FIGURE 17.2
Sam's page inspired by Jeff Kinney's Diary of a Wimpy Kid

Move to Make No. 24: Research favorite writers to connect with them as mentors.

Mentors for Poetry

As students get older, poets are often the mentors who nudge them to keep writing. Poems have the ability to lure minimal writers. I like to think poetry is like the force of gravity. Just as it is impossible not to feel the gravitational pull of the earth, it is impossible for young writers not to feel the pull of poetry.

Science buffs know that gravitational pull is a critical reason objects have potential energy. I think if we want to increase the potential of kids from hard places, we do well to tempt them with poetry. Poetry makes writing seem possible. It is short. It is playful. It is correct. (e. e. cummings even made capitalization optional for poets!)

Move to Make No. 25: Introduce students to poets as mentors.

Amy Ludwig VanDerwater is hands-down my favorite poet for students to get to know. Her blog *The Poem Farm* unlocks her process and is a treasure trove for writers of all ages. Amy loves poetry and kids, especially kids who write poetry, and will interact through blog comments and on Twitter.

One strength of using Amy's poetry as mentor texts is that she writes about ordinary things. She pays attention to the book stack on the back of the toilet and the animal tracks in the snow. She makes the everyday seem magical. When I need help enticing students to write, I print a few of Amy's delightful poems and let them loose in the classroom. It is impossible not to feel a writing pull when surrounded by Amy Ludwig VanDerwater's poetry.

Students also gravitate toward Mattie Stepanek. Mattie lost his battle with a rare form of muscular dystrophy when he was thirteen years old. Before his death, he was a bestselling author and speaker, publishing seven books in his short life. Not only is his poetry inspiring, but so is his story. His website is full of poems that can become mentor texts for students.

Other poets students are pulled toward include Eloise Greenfield, J. Patrick Lewis, and Lee Bennett Hopkins.

TAKING THE FIRST STEPS

- *Check out how other writers work by learning about their processes. Mary Helen Gensch curated a nice collection of author websites and videos about their approaches to the writing process (you can find it at https:// booksavors.wordpress.com/authors).*

- *Select a writer as your own mentor and be inspired. Pair your writing with the mentor text and plan to share it with your students.*

CHAPTER 18:
SIMPLIFY CONFERRING

One of the mantras that tends to roll around in my head as I'm working with writers is *Don't make it more complicated than it needs to be*. Teaching is complex. Kids are complex. Writing is complex. Teaching kids to write is complex.

This doesn't mean we have to make it more complicated than it needs to be. Conferring is the heart of teaching writers. When we sit together as one writer to another, important work can happen. Teachers learn what students need. Students grow as writers.

If you do a quick Google search of "writing workshop conferences" or "conferring notes," you will have more sites and images to wade through than you can possibly have time to read. This kind of search and deep dive into pretty PDFs is not the way to simplify conferences.

Instead, let's make a commitment to not make it more complicated than it needs to be. Following are key moves to make while conferring to entice students to write.

NAME STRENGTHS

We can entice students to write by identifying what they are doing well as writers. I've found that many students don't even know when they are making an effective craft move or using conventions properly. When we highlight what they are already doing well as writers, we build their confidence; when students are confident, they are more likely to want to write.

I invite Stephanie to write an entry in my digital writer's notebook. I hand her my phone; she types something and hands it back. I read what she wrote.

"Be still my heart! You've learned to use paragraphs!"

"I have?" Stephanie says.

I raise my eyebrows. "Are you joking? Here I am having heart palpitations from your paragraphs, and you didn't even know you used them?"

Stephanie giggles. "I guess not. Let me see."

I hand the phone back to her so she can reread her draft. "Oh yeah. I did that to make it easier to understand."

Stephanie isn't the exception. There are many times when students make a strong move as a writer and don't even know they've done it.

My oldest daughter Hannah wrote an essay about herself as a writer. These lines make me chuckle:

> *My weaknesses are that when my writing is done it tends to repeat a lot*
> *and is always the same things over and over again and can be redundant.*
> *I also tend to stray off the point. I say something then go to another thing*
> *that doesn't make any sense with what I am writing. I need help with*
> *introductions.*

"Why are you laughing?" asks Hannah.

"Were you being funny on purpose in this section?"

She looks over my shoulder. "Oh yeah, I used 'over and over' because that's like repeating words."

I laugh again. "The rest of it is repeating, too."

She rereads her words and smirks. "Oh yeah! It is! That's kind of funny."

"So's this part. You say you stray off the point and then you stray with the whole introduction bit."

"Yeah, I didn't mean to do that," she says, reading the part again. "I see what you mean, though. I guess I can add humor by overemphasizing my point."

My daughters aren't the only kids who need their strengths as writers pointed out. As you confer with your students, take time to highlight the things they are doing well as writers. Even the most basic writers have things you can acknowledge and build on as strengths.

Move to Make No. 26: Name the strengths students have as writers.

Strengths to Notice in Basic Writers

1. Meaningful topic choice. *If students select a topic that is personal, make sure to acknowledge it.*

2. Action or dialogue in narratives. *Many students are driven either by action or by dialogue.*

3. Solid facts in nonfiction. *Often students will "fact dump" when writing nonfiction. This can be highlighted as a strength.*

4. Passionate opinions. *Opinion writing can be difficult for some students to focus on, but a passionate opinion will bubble to the surface.*

5. Effective writing habits. *Notice the wise decisions students make as writers and point out how these decisions position them to write well.*

MAKE SURE TO TEACH

Talking with students about their strengths as writers does not complete a conference. In *How's It Going?* Carl Anderson (2000) describes conferences as conversations; in fact, one chapter is titled "Conferences Are Conversations." If we end the conversation after chatting about the student's strengths, then we are shortchanging the conversation.

This would be like if, during my post-evaluation conference, my assistant superintendent tells me all of the great things I do and then ends the conversation. Sure, I'm feeling good about myself, but I'm not positioned to grow. For the conference to be complete, the conversation must move beyond my strengths.

Solid conferences provide opportunities for growth. In writing conferences, this includes teaching points.

Like most instructional moves, this is easier said than done. For example, consider this conference with a fourth grader who dangles his "all done" story in front of my nose.

"I need to share this with everyone."

"Really? What makes you say that?"

His eyes grow wide. "Look at it! It's three pages and action packed! Remember you told me I'm an action-packed writer? I just kept writing more action since I'm so good at it."

◄ This student's self-confidence is critical to his success as a writer. I always take note of students who have confidence as writers.

I smile and take his draft to read it. "Wow, this *is* action packed," I say as I scan his story.

"I know!" he beams.

◀ Here I name his strength. The conference is just beginning. I need to continue in order to have a full conference and nudge growth in this student as a writer.

The action is abundant and the writer is proud, but this is a draft he was asked to revise because it had no internal story, no dialogue, no character names, no setting details, no paragraphs, no spaces between words, and very little ending punctuation. Instead of revising, he wants to read it to the class.

This is a difficult conversation to have while looking into the eyes of a young writer who is so full of faith in himself he's ready to receive the next Newbery Medal. Then we look down at the draft and wonder how he ever made it to fourth grade.

I know this isn't what I'm supposed to admit in a book about enticing writers, but the truth is that sometimes I wonder how I'm going to balance appreciating where students are in their development as writers and helping them to become more capable and confident in their craft. The answer always lies in a full conference.

I name another strength. This time it is about process rather than craft. Whenever I'm going to push a student out of his or her comfort zone, I pad the conversation ◀ with affirmations.

Returning to my action-packed writer, I point to the writing-process chart and say, "You're pretty good going through the top cycle—you have great ideas, make a plan (with lots of action!), and write a draft.

The thing is, writers write a whole lot more than they publish. It looks like you're the kind of writer who really loves to write first drafts."

◀ Then I move into teaching him about how writers work. It is part of the conversation, but the conversation has now shifted to teaching. Notice how this naturally continues through the remaining part of the conference.

I pause to judge his energy. He's nodding. I wait to see if he has anything to add to the conversation.

Wait time is ▶ important in a conference. Make sure to give a little quiet space.

"I kept thinking about the next part of my story while I was riding the bus to school," he says. "It's a little fun to write stories."

"I know. I love it when the characters start talking to me when I'm driving or doing the dishes. I know you're excited about sharing this with the whole world, but I think you should plan to share it with your writing group and then put it in your folder and start another draft."

He nods. "My writing group will like it. Then I can write another story about when we played football at my uncle's house."

I pause, because I'm a little confused. "Who played football at your uncle's house?"

"Me and my brother."

"Is that who was in your last story?"

"Yeah," he says. The word hangs in the air, almost transforming into *Duh!* before reaching my ears.

"I didn't know because you never used their names in this story."

He wrinkles his brow and pulls the draft out of my hand. He scans the story.

"That's weird," he says. "Writers usually name their characters." (This was one of last week's teaching points.)

"They do," I agree.

"I think I'll change that before I take it to writing group."

I smile at this small victory. "Maybe when you write your next story you can also use spaces between your words. I think it would really help your readers."

> ◄ I wouldn't count this as a teaching point for the conference. It is something the student realized, not something I was intentional about teaching.

He squints at his draft, looking for where to add character names.

"It'd help me, too," he says. "This isn't much fun to try and read."

I chuckle. "Remember the writing process and how we're going to write several drafts before Selection Day. Writers can't publish everything they write. They have to select their best stuff. For you maybe it's this draft, or maybe it's the next one."

> ◄ I almost left out this part of the conversation. It's important to focus on one teaching point in a conference. Yet, the reality of conversations is that they unfold organically. Because he was having a hard time reading his draft, it was a perfect time to mention using spaces between his words.

> I wrap up ► the conference by restating my main teaching point. The conversation was fluid, and I want to leave him with the next tasks clearly defined.

I'd love to report that the next draft was beautiful, with spaces between the words and paragraphs and ending punctuation. *It wasn't.* What I *can* say is that the student produced another story and then another and another. He was a capable and confident writer all year, and by June he exhibited marked progress in his drafts. They continued to be action packed (with a little bit of internal story) and quite readable.

Move to Make No. 27: Be intentional about teaching one main point in every conference.

OFFER A MEASURABLE CHALLENGE

After teaching in a conference, I often issue a challenge to help determine whether the student is engaging with the teaching point. In the previous conference, I would have asked to see the beginning of a new draft. Following are some challenges I return to again and again.

Writing Words

I am often motivated by word count when writing a first draft. I'm not alone. The popular NaNoWriMo is a novel-writing challenge devoted to word count. Word count is a measurable way to see your progress as a writer.

One way to challenge students is to ask them how far down a page they can write. I usually point to a spot a couple of lines down a page and say, "Do you think you can write to this point by the end of writing workshop today?"

I gauge the reaction. If students seem confident, I drop down a few more lines and ask, "What about here? Could you write to here?"

We agree on a point and make a mark in the margin. This is a way for basic writers to develop fluency. At the end of workshop, I check back in and celebrate the amount of writing my students complete.

Highlighters

Another challenge is to use highlighters to mark a specific craft move. For example, for narrative writing, ask students to highlight the internal story. Another option is to ask students to put a box around each part or scene so they can see which ones might need more development.

In nonfiction writing, students may use highlighters to code the different kinds of details—for example, yellow for facts, blue for asides, and orange for anecdotes. I remember a former student using highlighters in this way for her feature article. After she completed highlighting, she realized she had never used the yellow highlighter. In an informational article, she didn't have a single fact! This helped her determine what she should do during revision.

Plan to Report

During many conferences, I will ask a student to plan to share at the end of workshop. I explain to the student, "What we've talked about during this conference would be really useful for others to hear. Will you try this and then report to the class during the share?"

This is helpful both in determining whether the student understood the conference teaching point and in transforming the share session to a teaching opportunity.

Move to Make No. 28: Offer a measurable challenge for trying out the teaching point.

INCREASE ENERGY FOR WRITING

It's always fun to increase the energy a student has for the writing work ahead. Because kids are learning and growing as writers, there are always things they can work on to become stronger writers. Becoming stronger isn't easy. It takes hard work and dedication. Conferences include teaching points and challenges, so students are expected to do more writing work. If we are going to ask students to do more writing work, let's also increase their energy for the work.

In addition to celebrating and naming strengths, we can increase students' writing energy during the conference in the following ways.

Listen

In the classic novel *To Kill a Mockingbird*, Atticus Finch says, "If you just learn a single trick, Scout, you'll get along a lot better with all kinds of folks. You never really understand a person until you consider things from his point of view . . . until you climb inside of his skin and walk around in it" (1960, 39). Harper Lee understood that it's not just listening that is important to understanding another person's story—empathy is also essential.

Conferring provides a unique opportunity for us to listen to and understand the stories students tell. The simple act of listening sends a powerful message. Not only does it help us, as teachers, to better understand our students, but it also increases their energy.

Consider the last time you felt that someone listened to you in a genuine way. If that person asked you to do something, you were probably more likely to have energy for the task at hand. I know this is true for me.

Recently I wrote a series of articles about coaching. My editor called, and we had a conversation about my drafts. Instead of having me unfold the article in a chronological way, she asked me to craft a narrative. "Tell the story," she said.

This was going to require a substantial amount of time, yet I had energy for it. She listened to my story, understood my struggles, gave me direction, and then asked me to do a ton of work.

It doesn't really make sense to be excited about doing more work. Yet, when writers feel listened to, their energy for writing increases.

Move to Make No. 29: Increase students' energy levels for writing by listening with empathy.

Ask Questions

Asking questions goes hand in hand with listening well. When we ask questions, we give students the opportunity to tell more and to find the important parts of their writing work. Teachers often struggle with knowing what to ask in a writing conference. Figure 18.1 shows my go-to list of questions. Use this handy list when you are conferring with students. It will help you steer the conversation to what students are doing as writers and position you to teach to the point of need.

FIGURE 18.1
Conferring questions

How's it going?
What are you working on as a writer?
Tell me more.
What's going well?
What do you wish you knew as a writer?
Tell me more.
Will you tell me about this part?
What would you be doing if I didn't interrupt you?
Tell me more.

A printable version of this list can be found here: https://drive.google.com/file/d/0ByOZHIxyJ7nT3o1MnVVVzBLUWs/view?usp=sharing).

The repeated statement on the list—"Tell me more"—is my favorite way to keep the conversation going and to increase students' energy for writing. When we say "Tell me more" to students, we are allowing them to set the direction of the conversation. We are also making the positive presupposition that they have more to say. Whenever I'm stuck on what to say in a writing conference, I tend to use this line. It is a powerful way to increase students' writing energy.

> Move to Make No. 30: Increase students' energy for writing by asking open-ended questions while conferring.

Check In and Share

When we check in with each student who's had a conference, we help increase his or her energy for writing. Once students know you care enough to see how they are doing *after* a conference, they thrive from the accountability. This gives students a chance to share their new work with you, and it allows you to make adjustments to your teaching so students have a clear understanding of the teaching point.

When students execute the teaching point in a conference, I often ask to use their work as an example for the rest of the class. This is another way to increase writing energy. Most students enjoy seeing their work highlighted in a mini-lesson. This also allows other students to better access the teaching point because they see it in a peer's work.

Another option is to share work during share sessions. Social media is a powerful way to share students' learning from conferences too.

> **Move to Make No. 31: Develop the habit of checking in with students after a conference and sharing their work with others.**

TAKING THE FIRST STEPS

- *Make a copy of the list of strengths to notice in basic writers and keep it handy when you are conferring with students. Return to it and name a specific strength for each student you confer with this week.*

- *Pay attention to the questions you are asking in your conferences. Use the list of questions to provide students the opportunity to lead the conversation.*

- *Take time for a self-check at the end of each conference. Do your students seem to have more or less energy for writing after talking with you? Do you have more or less energy for teaching writing after the conference? Home in on ways to increase the energy for writing in your classroom.*

CHAPTER 19:
EXPAND FEEDBACK
BEYOND THE TEACHER

n fourth grade, Jordan pulls a memoir out of his backpack. Notebook paper is pasted to a sheet of red construction paper. The edges are crinkled and rolled. "You've gotta read this, Mom!" he announces, shoving the writing under my nose.

I take the writing. "The other kids loved it," Jordan says. "They laughed when I read it to them. No one made people laugh more than me."

Jordan rides this energy wave for the remainder of the year in writing workshop. Because he got positive feedback from his classmates, he's on fire for writing.

Since feedback is a powerful tool in developing confident writers, it is important for students to receive feedback from more people than just the teacher. There are many ways we can advocate additional feedback for students.

END-OF-WORKSHOP SHARE SESSIONS

The end-of-workshop share session is an expected part of each day and makes a great time for students to engage with sharing their writing.

Move to Make 32: Diversify the end of workshop share sessions to provide more opportunities for students to share and hear about their writing.

In Figure 19.1, you will find several different kinds of share sessions to close your writing workshop. I am an advocate for diversity in share sessions. I think it is good for students to share in a variety of ways and with a variety of people. The common thread in all share sessions is the opportunity for students to cheer and challenge one another. This is how confidence is boosted and students are enticed to write.

FIGURE 19.1

A variety of share sessions to build students' confidence as writers

TYPE	DESCRIPTION
High Five	*Students find a partner by giving someone a high five. They share a small part of their writing with each other. Then they put their hands up to find another partner to high five.*
Gallery Walk	*Students walk around the classroom looking at each other's writing (or parts of writing).*
Partner	*Students sit with a partner and share their writing.*
Small Group	*Students share in a group of 3-5 students.*
Author Chair	*One student shares his or her writing with the whole class.*
Teaching Share	*One student teaches something he or she has learned as a writer to the whole class.*
Whip Share	*Students sit in a circle and prepare to share a line from their writing. Students "whip" around the circle, each sharing one line.*
Social Media Share	*Students share their learning and their goals on a social network.*

CHEER & CHALLENGE

Although there is much opportunity to build confidence during a share session, there is also potential for harm. When we share our writing, we are vulnerable.

Let's find opportunities to use the share session to challenge the listeners rather than the writer. The writer is already in the spotlight. If we can cheer the writer and challenge the writing community, then our share sessions become invaluable confidence boosters for every child in the room.

Take a look at the table in Figure 19.1. For each type of share, consider how you could cheer on the writer and challenge the writing community in your classroom. In some cases, the cheer is a high five or a special clap. Let's not belittle this kind of cheer. Fist bumps can fuel writers. In other cases, the cheer is identifying what the writer is doing well.

One way to tie the cheer and challenge together is to ask, "What did you notice someone else doing as a writer that you would like to try, too?" This allows another student to be celebrated while someone else is being challenged to try something as a writer.

Move to Make No. 33: Offer feedback that will both cheer and challenge writers.

BUILDING CONFIDENCE TOGETHER

Writers need confidence to be willing to write. It is too easy to believe that our stories don't matter and our writing is bad. I think part of writing well is learning to slay the monsters in our minds. I like to draw a picture of the writing monsters in my head for students (see Figure 19.2).

The monsters in my head like to tell me lies. They say things like, "Your writing is stupid. You were lucky to write one book, and you'll never do it again. If you can't remember whether you need an apostrophe in *its*, what makes you think you should be a writer?"

It's important for students to know that writers have to fight these lies. I invite students to tell me the lies their writing monsters tell them. Sometimes we draw our writing monsters in our notebooks and write the lies that they whisper to us.

Fortunately, we also have "Little Writers" in our minds. I like to imagine a miniature me with a ginormous pencil slaying the writing monsters (see Figure 19.3). This Little Writer reminds me of the things I do well as a writer. She helps me add the five senses to make my writing more descriptive or use more specific words to make a stronger picture for the reader. The Little Writer can tell the writing monsters to be quiet.

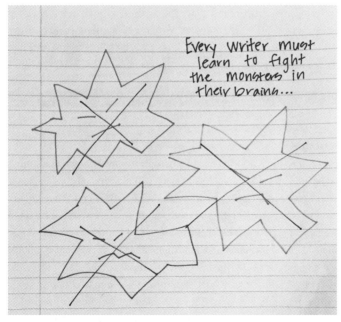

Every writer must learn to fight the monsters in their brains...

FIGURE 19.2
The writing monsters in my head

FIGURE 19.3
The Little Writer who helps quiet the writing monsters

A community develops as we share our struggles and fears. We become stronger when we do this. Giving students time to share the mental battle of being a writer helps entice them to write. My confidence as a writer is higher because of my relationships with other writers. They cheer me on and challenge me to grow. We can help students reap these benefits, too.

Move to Make No. 34: Provide time for students to share the mental battle of being a writer.

Corralling Feedback

In order to hold on to the positive effects of feedback, we need to make as much of it tangible as possible. After a conversation with Bill, my editor, I write down his suggestions *and* I record the things he likes about my work. I add these notes to my writer's notebook. My *Choice Literacy* editor, Brenda, always sends me a note after she receives an article. Many of these notes I add to my notebook. They serve as affirmations of why I keep writing. When Brenda and I meet or talk on the phone, I take a few minutes to write down the highlights of our conversations.

When I met with my friend, Pastor Kurt Stout, to talk about sharing my story on a Sunday morning, I wrote notes about our conversation. Although I recorded questions and jotted down ideas to think more about, I also noted what Kurt liked and the positive feedback he offered.

I use my notebook to corral feedback. We can teach students to do this, too. When they receive feedback, they can add it to their notebooks. This helps them to grow as writers. It is always helpful to know what people appreciate about our writing so we can do it again and again. It also helps to see how the feedback changes over time.

Move to Make No. 35: Use writing notebooks to collect written feedback.

The following table lists people who can offer feedback to students. Encourage them to take time to write a note for students to add to their notebooks. Alternatively, teach students how to write down the feedback they receive from others to add to their notebooks. I often use a sticky note during the conversation so I don't forget the good stuff I'm told about my writing.

AUDIENCE	NOTES TO LEAVE
Classmates	Take advantage of a comment sheet during a celebration and give students the opportunity to leave short notes for one another.
School Staff	When you post student writing or invite adults in the school to a celebration, hand out little note sheets and ask visitors to write a few words of encouragement to students. I love using preprinted notepads for these notes.
Family Members	Send home a notecard in an envelope on the day published writing goes home. Ask a family member to write a kind note about the child's writing, seal it in the envelope, and return it to school. Students can open notes and add them to their writing notebooks as another celebration and reminder of their strengths as writers.

"We all need people who will give us feedback. That's how we improve."
–Bill Gates

TAKING THE FIRST STEPS

- *Use the video minilesson* Cheer and Challenge *to find the words to nudge students to offer encouraging and constructive feedback.*

- *Share your students' writing work on social media. As students receive feedback, invite them to record it in their notebooks to access later.*

- *Snap some pictures as students share their writing with an audience. Print these pictures and add them to your classroom or bulletin boards with student writing. If printing is easy, print an extra copy of pictures for students to add to their notebooks. The smiles in the pictures offer encouragement to writers on their hardest days.*

- *Create a place to capture feedback from others about student writing. Find a bulletin board or create a space near the writing center. A title such as*

Our Writing Affects Others *or* What People Say About Our Writing *helps to position the space as something you can use over and over. Use speech bubbles to record feedback about student writing. I prefer to have these accessible to students to take with their published writing and give to their audiences. It's one of those things students typically return because they enjoy adding feedback to the board. Watch for students who don't have feedback on the board and tap other teachers, the principal, or support staff to read and respond to a recent project.*

CHAPTER 20:
TAP TECHNOLOGY

Hannah and Stephanie are learning to knit hats over Christmas break. When they forget how to finish a hat, they use FaceTime to confer with Aunt Becky. Soon the hat stacks are rivaling the book stacks in our house. As a break from knitting, the girls begin crocheting ear warmers and flowers for accents. They find instructions on YouTube and Pinterest. They take over one of the cabinets under the bookshelves to store yarn. Finally, I ask them: "What are you going to do with all of these hats and ear warmers?"

"We should sell them," Stephanie says. She already has the heart of an entrepreneur.

"What would you do with the money?" I ask.

Hannah answers before Stephanie. "I know! We should give it to kids in foster care. Things are hard for them. We could use the money to get them things like suitcases."

"Suitcases would be good," Stephanie agrees. "Then they don't have to show up to their forever family with things in garbage bags."

"Yeah, that's kind of embarrassing," Hannah says.

The girls are silent and continue looping yarn into warm hats.

Stephanie says, "I'd like to help other kids, too. Not just kids in foster care, but kids in other countries. Like Jose, who gets to go to school because we adopted him—well, kind of adopted, not like our adoption, but we invest in him. Maybe we can give money to some other orphans, too."

"Vulnerable children," Hannah says. "Remember, that's a better term than orphan."

I love these girls. It's a moment when I wonder how I'm lucky enough to be their mom. "How much of the profit would you want to give away?"

"All of it," Hannah says.

Stephanie agrees. "Sure, all of it. We have everything we need."

They begin dreaming of their business. Hannah gets a notebook and organizes their thoughts. Warmed by Love is created.

"We need an Instagram account," Hannah says. "That's how people will find us."

Within moments, she establishes an Instagram account. The girls research prices and how to photograph the items. We spend a Sunday afternoon learning about opening an Etsy shop. Stephanie and Hannah take pictures and discuss captions. I teach them to use Photoshop and a little about logos.

They are sharing their messages in a multitude of ways, through Instagram and Facebook and Etsy, class presentations and locker posters and e-mails to local businesses, captions and tags and business cards. Knowing how to share their message has become essential.

This isn't only true for my children, but for the kids sitting in our classrooms, too. They are authoring texts. If we are going to entice students to write, then it's time to embrace technology in our writing workshops.

TECHNOLOGY AS A TOOL

Just like writing notebooks, sticky notes, or colored pens, technology is a tool for writers. Like all tools, it can be used to help or hinder.

I love to cook. There are many tools I use to make my time in the kitchen more efficient and enjoyable. The strawberry huller, meat mallet, and garlic press are all tools I use as a cook. However, when my sons get ahold of these items, they do not make time in the kitchen more efficient or enjoyable. Just because they have access to these tools doesn't mean they use them to enhance the cooking experience. In fact, I would contend that a meat mallet in the hands of a ten-year-old boy is rarely a good idea.

Let's consider the ways technology can entice students to grow as writers.

Write About

Write About is a social publishing platform. It was created by Brad Wilson and John Spencer, two teachers who wanted to help students to grow as writers, along with Bob Armbrister, whose technology and business experience rounded out the partnership. They've developed a team that believes "writing should be fun and sharing should be easy, so they built a digital writing platform for classrooms" (https://www.writeabout.com).

Since it is a tool developed by teachers who understand that the way students grow as writers is to write, Write About isn't filled with gimmicks to manipulate students. Rather, it builds on the core beliefs of writing workshop and provides a place for students to become fluent writers and engage as a community of people who write.

Move to Make No. 36: Select technology tools and apps that support the core beliefs of writing workshop.

I admire the way Write About uses images to inspire student writers. Images are an essential part of communication in today's world and drive most of our interactions online. Write About has thousands of freely available visual writing ideas. Plus, teachers can create their own images to share with students. The topics in Write About range from soccer to social justice and everything in between. The images spark ideas for the gamut of types of writing—narrative, informative, argument, and poetry.

Write About is a good option for a digital writing notebook. The posts can be used as quick writes to develop fluency, and there are metrics, such as word count, to help students keep track of their activity as writers. Just as we add all kinds of ephemera to our paper writing notebooks, Write About has many options for students. There are images, audio capabilities, and font choices.

Write About encourages a strong writing community. It is a digital option for organizing writing partners or groups. It allows for students to safely give, receive, and track feedback. Often it is difficult for some students to connect in writing partnerships or groups. The online nature of Write About helps ease some of the fears some students have about interacting with others. These connections often lead students to develop a stronger drive to write and share their words.

In *Engaging Students with Poverty in Mind* (2013), Eric Jensen cites some sobering statistics shared by Betty Hart and Todd Risley. He writes:

> In poor homes, the ratio of positives (affirmations) to negatives (reprimands) is typically a 1-to-2 ratio. Contrast this to the 6-to-1 positives-to-negatives ratio in the homes of higher-income families (1995). (15)

Write About offers an opportunity for students to receive affirmation about their writing through comments. Students learn to accept this positive feedback and new pathways are established in their brains. In addition, as they offer encouraging feedback to other students, relationships are strengthened.

There is a free version of Write About, so go ahead and try it out with your students who are hesitant to write. It's one way to dip your toes into using technology to increase motivation, fluency, and feedback.

Interview with Brad Wilson, Chief Operations Officer of Write About

RUTH: *How does having a digital option for notebook entries entice kids to write?*

BRAD: *Students are already learners in a digital world. They will be digital writers for the rest of their lives. We don't know what devices and platforms they will be on, but it's clear that they will need to communicate effectively using technology. It's our job to help students view themselves as writers—no matter what space they are in, no matter how they input text, no matter what media elements coincide with the text. Giving them the power to publish and see themselves as digital authors is an essential part of today's writing process.*

RUTH: *How does offering students image choices entice them to write?*

BRAD: *Choice is a big motivator for many young writers. Digital environments allow teachers to provide them with more choices about the topics they choose, the multimedia they use, and the audience they publish to. Images hook students for any genre. Just look at how graphical the web is: Instagram, Pinterest, PBS Kids—you name it. Visuals drive our interactions online. Why not leverage powerful imagery to get students thinking, drafting, and responding?*

RUTH: *How would you encourage teachers to keep looking for ways to empower kids to write?*

BRAD: *We should be referring to all forms of writing as just that—writing. Don't call it "tweeting" or "blogging." Instead, we can say, "What did you write on your tweet?" or, "Who will be your audience for your narrative post?" The conversations about the choices that authors make no longer need to be hypothetical because, chances are, your students are already authoring digital content.*

RUTH: *That's so true! I agree that it is important to expand our definition of writing to include all instances of using words to communicate a message or story. How do you see audience as a factor in enticing students to write?*

BRAD: *Audience and the social elements in a digital writing community are a big hook for students. When they have opportunities to publish to their peers, we see motivation increase and students write more. With practice, modeling and feedback, students not only transfer their offline writing skills to these new spaces . . . but their writing actually gets better! It's almost magical when you see reluctant writers find their voice and naturally utilize their new skills . . . and getting that to happen for more kids requires that we meet them in their [digital] world.*

RUTH: *Yes, that moment when it seems magical—we all love it! Thanks, Brad, for all you do to entice students to write and to make a social publishing platform manageable for teachers!*

BRAD: *Thank you. It has been my pleasure.*

Google Drive

Google Drive has become integral to my writing life. Rarely do I work on something outside of Drive. I'm grateful for how easy it is to organize files, view the history of a document, and collaborate with others on the platform. It has transformed the way I work as a writer.

Sam's Google Drive is robust. He has folders for different topics he researches—trains, oil spills, helicopters, dogs, and much more. There are folders for different writing projects—his graphic novel *Toilet Man,* skateboard shoes, retractable dog leashes, faith, and life stories. He has a folder for blog posts where he captures lists of ideas, snippets of writing, and pictures.

If students have Google accounts, then their writing lives can also be transformed with Google Drive. Drive provides a stable place to keep and save writing projects. It is special to keep writing projects over time, and Drive makes this possible. For students from hard places, keeping work over time is usually impossible. With Drive, no longer is keeping your history as a writer dependent on having a parent who will lovingly store all your sweet writing projects.

Google Drive allows teachers to add technology to writing workshop in an organic way. The key is to offer invitations to students to use technology as writers. For example, after you show students how to use a storyboard as a way to plan, you can offer this invitation: "If you have another way to plan the scenes of your narrative, feel free to give it a try."

Be open to new possibilities for students to plan scenes. Some may want to use sticky notes instead of a storyboard. Others may decide to use Google Slides to create a digital version of a storyboard. Each time I offer an invitation to students to expand on a tool I've shared, I'm always enamored by their creativity. It is important to remember it isn't the tool but the process that is valuable to writers.

You can offer invitations as often or as little as you like. If your students have access to their own devices, then I would encourage you to do so as often as possible. Technology is power, and it is especially important for kids from hard places.

Just as they do with craft and conventions, students will make approximations about how to use technology as writers. Value these approximations and remember to consider what students are *almost* doing as writers. Once we are able to identify the approximations, then we can help students use technology in more efficient and useful ways.

Social Media

In Daniel Pink's TED Talk, "Drive," he shares a story of two companies developing an encyclopedia. In the 1990s, Microsoft paid a renowned team top dollar to create the Encarta Encyclopedia. Everyone thought it was going to be timeless.

Meanwhile, another group began an encyclopedia. It was free. Anyone could add information to it; you didn't have to be an expert, and you weren't paid to contribute.

Wikipedia continues to grow today. Encarta is dusty.

Who knew something free and collaborative would become timeless? Although Wikipedia may not be around forever, the collaborative nature of social media will be. Humans are social beings. We like to interact, and we love to grow our knowledge.

Social media is a way of life. Nearly everyone is connected on some platform. My friend Joe, who's over eighty, is a social media guru. He loves that he can stay connected through online spaces. Joe follows me on Twitter, tries to get me to interact more on Facebook, and likes to Skype with me on Sundays, whether he is in town or on the other side of the globe. If my friend Joe is connected on social media, there's a good chance you are, too.

There's an even better chance that our students are connected (or want desperately to be connected, depending on the places they are coming from). When we use social media to entice writers, we are not only harnessing positive energy for writing, but we are also teaching important lessons for interacting in online communities.

Social media is part of our lives, and it is important to a contemporary writing life. We do not operate in isolation. Social media allows us to gather research, receive support from other writers, and interact with our audiences. Social media is not something we ought to do *to* our students. In order for it to be authentic, we must engage with social media as professionals.

Unless we connect via social media, we miss a chance to model for students the ease and importance of collaboration. As an introvert, I was frozen by the thought of interacting on social media for years. I started as a blogger with a small audience and always imagine writing to a handful of people. When I joined Twitter, I was petrified. First, I didn't understand the platform. I was clueless and didn't want to make a mistake. Next, I wasn't sure if I could just join in a conversation or if that was a Twitter *faux pas*. After a few days, I realized I just needed to tweet. I dove in and was amazed at the warm welcome the community gave me.

Across social media, educators provide a warm welcome to others who are stepping into a platform for the first time. This is true for those who join the CELEBRATE This Week community on my blog, *Ruth Ayres Writes*. (I've helped hundreds of people start blogging, and to a person they were pleasantly surprised by the support and encouragement they found in the blogging community.) It is true for Tweeps ("Twitter peeps") who are just starting to tweet. It is true on Instagram. I've yet to find a social media platform where educators have not extended a warm welcome to others in the field.

Move to Make No. 37: Leverage social media to entice students to write.

Consider your journey with social media. How have you evolved? By taking time to reflect on the impact social media has on your life, you will be able to envision ways to use it to entice students to write. Consider the following chart and think about how each stage looked (or looks) in your own life.

SOCIAL MEDIA CONTINUUM

No social media connections	*Most of us need to think back to a time when we didn't have social media connections. (Even my grandma is connected, however loosely: She loves to see my Instagram posts when my mom visits her.) It's wild to think that many of our students will never remember a time without social media!*
Use social media in personal life	*At this stage, you interact on social media strictly on a personal level. You might not even connect with friends from work!*
Branching out to use social media as a professional	*You read blogs from other educators and follow other teachers, classrooms, or people in the field on Twitter, Facebook, or another platform. You share favorite articles, links, or posts. Sometimes you engage in a professional conversation, but mostly you lurk.*
Use social media as a professional	*You engage with a professional learning community (PLC) online and turn to it for information, support, and encouragement. You begin to connect your classroom with families by sharing announcements via social media and (maybe) pictures from the school day.*
Provide opportunities for students to interact on social media	*You connect your classroom to a social media platform to share learning experiences with others. Students determine the content they share and may (depending on a variety of circumstances) be responsible for sharing their own content.*
Intentionally step into new social media platforms	*Social media is always evolving. It's easy to become comfortable with one platform and never move beyond it. At this stage, you seek to experience dipping into a new platform.*

THE PRIVILEGE OF TECHNOLOGY

People are writing more today than at any other time in history. As students realize that their stories matter and their messages make a difference, we want to be in position to encourage them to reach beyond the walls of their classrooms. Technology allows us this privilege.

Students are learning to compose texts on devices. Although the writing process remains the same, the tools to execute each phase are evolving. Many kids, like Hannah and Stephanie, have families that support their stories and empower them to share their messages online. However, there are others who do not have this encouragement. As we embrace technology, we can entice all writers to share their messages and make a difference in the lives of others.

TAKING THE FIRST STEPS

- *Sign your classroom up for a Twitter account! You will find all kinds of fascinating facts and be able to interact with many classroom-friendly authors. You will also find other classrooms and be able to connect with educators around the globe. I prefer to use Twitter as a closure to writing workshop (or any part of the school day) by asking students, "What did we learn or experience that we should share with our followers?" It is a powerful (and simple) reflection and a super formative assessment.*

- *Consider students in your class who are hesitant to write and take the time to set up a Write About account for them. Give them time to collect entries and interact with others in the writing community.*

- *Tap the power of the camera app. Students can collect photos or videos. They can create digital texts. They are able to save memories, experiences, and learning with a quick tap on the screen. The old saying "A picture is worth a thousand words" may literally be true when it comes to today's writers. I know I often write a thousand words based on a single photo! A camera app has a place in writing workshop. In fact, I believe we will soon find it nearly impossible to work as writers without one.*

CLOSING THOUGHTS: PRESS ON

didn't plan on writing a circular ending for this book, but life has a way of turning around on itself sometimes and ignoring our best-laid plans. Last week I wrote these words in my notebook:

I might want to quit today.

I'm tired. My head hurts. I'm too cold. I'm too hot. I feel pudgy. I can't seem to please a single person (except Andy, but that's just because love is blind).

I'm tired of hearing teachers talk about "these kids" and how they just need a little discipline and a lot of love. As if you can make a kid from trauma play within logical boundaries. As if a warm hug is enough to soothe a kid who comes from a hard place.

There are some days I'm glad I have my notebook because I can write the hard things and try to make sense of them. I wish there weren't so many kids living in hard places.

If I knew this was going to be a circular story, I wouldn't have begun with fake fingernails and handcuffs. It was funny when I wrote it. I hope you laughed.

I stack words in my notebook and Stephanie sits in jail. Twelve years old, and the police took her away in handcuffs. There isn't anything fake about it.

If I knew this was going to be a circular story, I may have reconsidered writing this book. I dip into the writing and attempt to tame my story lines of momma, educator, and writer. Without fail, each time I find a bit of traction, things fall apart with Stephanie.

This happens when kids come from hard places. This happens when we walk alongside those who are trying to overcome a history of hard.

If I knew this was going to be a circular story, I wonder if I would change my stance on anything. I've reread the entire manuscript through the eyes of someone who is tattered from loving people with hard histories. It's not easy living alongside broken people.

You know, because you do it, too. It's part of the job of being a teacher—we live alongside broken people. We try to make one corner of the world a little brighter, to give hope and offer healing. It's not easy, and sometimes we feel tattered.

Now that I know this is a circular story—beginning and ending with handcuffs—I realize there's not a single thing I would change. I still believe teachers save and stories change the world. I still believe our most important work is to offer students a voice and the ability to rewrite their stories.

Enticing students to write is about finding the line between enabling and empowering. It's a hard line to find when kids are in dark places. This book is about understanding the hard places kids come from and then finding ways to uplift them. As you take leaps of faith and make moves to entice kids to write, may you also know there will come a time when "these kids" will almost get the best of you.

You might want to quit on that day.

Don't do it.

Instead, take the time to see their stories. Remember, you have the power to change the course of lives. All children deserve to know that they can write a different version of their stories.

Fight the good fight. It might be hard, but it is worth it.

Press on, brave teacher.

References

Anderson, Carl. 2000. *How's It Going? A Practical Guide to Conferring with Student Writers*. Portsmouth, NH: Heinemann.

Anderson, Jeff. 2007. *Everyday Editing*. Portland, ME: Stenhouse.

——. 2005. *Mechanically Inclined*. Portland, ME: Stenhouse.

Ayres, Ruth. *Ruth Ayres Writes*. http://www.ruthayreswrites.com.

Ayres, Ruth, with Christi Overman. 2012. *Celebrating Writers*. Portland, ME: Stenhouse.

Behnke, Ramona. *Pleasures from the Page*. http://pleasuresfromthepage.blogspot.com.

Calkins, Lucy. 1994. *The Art of Teaching Writing*. Portsmouth, NH: Heinemann.

Cruz, Colleen. 2004. *Independent Writing: One Teacher—Thirty-Two Needs, Topics, and Plans*. Portsmouth, NH: Heinemann.

Daniels, Harvey, Steven Zemelman, and Nancy Steineke. 2007. *Content-Area Writing: Every Teacher's Guide*. Portsmouth, NH: Heinemann.

Day, Deb. *Coffee With Chloe*. http://deb-day.blogspot.com.

DiCamillo, Kate. 2002. *The Tiger Rising*. New York: Scholastic.

Fletcher, Ralph. 2002. *Poetry Matters*. New York: Harper Collins.

——. 2000. *How Writers Work: Finding a Process That Works for You*. New York: Harper Collins.

Fletcher, Ralph, and JoAnn Portalupi. 2001. *Writing Workshop: The Essential Guide*. Portsmouth, NH: Heinemann.

Fox, Mem. 1993. *Radical Reflections: Passionate Opinions on Teaching, Learning, and Living*. San Diego, CA: Harcourt Brace.

Gensch, Mary Helen. *Book Savors*. https://booksavors.wordpress.com.

Graves, Don, and Penny Kittle. 2005. *Inside Writing: How to Teach the Details of Craft*. Portsmouth, NH: Heinemann.

Heard, Georgia. 2014. *The Revision Toolbox.* Portsmouth, NH: Heinemann.

Jensen, Eric. 2013. *Engaging Students with Poverty in Mind.* Alexandria, VA: ASCD.

Kittle, Penny. 2008. *Write Beside Them.* Portsmouth, NH: Heinemann.

Lane, Barry. 2015. *After the End.* Portsmouth, NH: Heinemann.

Lee, Harper. 1960. *To Kill a Mockingbird.* New York: Harper Perennial Modern Classics.

Ludwig VanDerwater, Amy. *The Poem Farm.* www.poemfarm.amylv.com.

Messner, Kate. 2011. *Real Revision.* Portland, ME: Stenhouse.

Miller, Donald. 2009. *A Million Miles in a Thousand Years: How I Learned to Live a Better Story.* Nashville, TN: Thomas Nelson.

Murray, Donald. 1981. "Making Meaning Clear: The Logic of Revision." *Journal of Basic Writing* 3 (3), 33–40.

Pink, Daniel. "The Puzzle of Motivation." https://www.ted.com/talks/dan_pink_on_motivation.

Romano, Tom. 2015. *Write What Matters: For Yourself, For Others.* Bristol, UK: Zigzag.

—. 1987. *Clearing the Way: Working with Teenage Writers.* Portsmouth, NH: Heinemann.

Urban, Linda. 2009. *A Crooked Kind of Perfect.* Boston: HMH Books for Young Readers.

Wong, Harry. 2004. *The First Days of School.* Mountain View, CA: Harry K. Wong.

Yolen, Jane. 2006. *Take Joy: A Writer's Guide to Loving the Craft.* Fairfield, OH: Writer's Digest Books.